W9-BLU-579

Amp'd

A FATHER'S BACKSTAGE PASS

GARY FINCKE

Michigan State University Press · *East Lansing*

Copyright © 2004 by Gary Fincke

⊗ The paper used in this publication meets the minimum requirements of ANSI/NISO
Z39.48-1992 (R 1997) (Permanence of Paper).

 Michigan State University Press
East Lansing, Michigan 48823-5245

Printed and bound in the United States of America.

10 09 08 07 06 05 04   1 2 3 4 5 6 7 8 9 10

LIBRARY OF CONGRESS CATALOGING-IN-PUBLICATION DATA
Fincke, Gary.
Amp'd : a father's backstage pass / Gary Fincke.
p. cm.
ISBN 0-87013-729-8 (pbk. : alk. paper)
1. Fincke, Aaron. 2. Rock musicans—United States—Biography. 3. Rock music—United
States—History and criticism. 4. Popular culture—United States. I. Title.
ML419.F55F56 2004
787.87'166'092—dc22
2004012337

Cover design by Heather Truelove Aiston
Book design by Sharp Designs, Inc., Lansing, Michigan

Cover photo is used courtesy of the photographer, © 2004 Thomas Bonomo.

Visit Michigan State University Press on the World Wide Web at *www.msupress.msu.edu*

for

Strangers With Candy,

    Lifer, Breaking Benjamin,

        and especially for Aaron

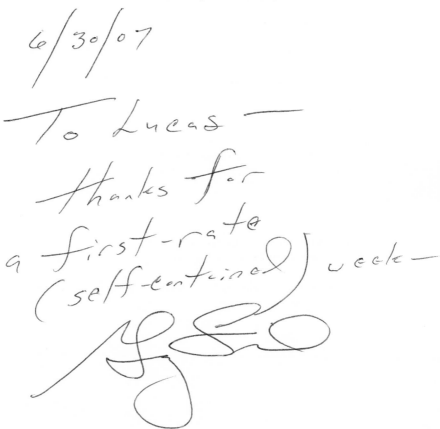

Luke,
It's been a pleasure!
I look forward to seeing
you in print someday!,
Patrick F. Blaney

6/30/07

To Lucas —
thanks for
a first-rate
(self-contained) week —

Contents

kicking ass

"Could these guys kick anymore ass? NO!" — Gina, a fan

Four women in front of me, four women in back, and every one wears skin-tight leather pants and a black sleeveless halter top that says *candy girls* in the same font style as the official logo for Strangers With Candy. The line to get into the club lurches forward, and their words rise and fall, shaped by the size and rhythm of their breasts.

All of them have IDs in their right hands and cigarettes in their left, and all of them look thin and a touch too haggard for women in their twenties. "I'm on the guest list," I say to one of the two women taking six dollars from everybody in the line.

She peeks at her guest list sheet, then looks me up and down, repeating to herself, I imagine, that maybe I'm someone other than a rock band fan because I'm twice the age of nearly everyone who's passed by her this evening. "Name?" she says, and I give it, but without glancing down again, she says, "I don't see it."

I force a smile. I feel an elbow jolt against my back and see all eight of the Candy Girls rush to the front of the stage, arranging themselves two-deep between two burly men who look as if they've just finished a six-month regimen of bench presses and steroids. They all lean forward as if the show has already begun, and then two push themselves up and head toward the bar. "My son plays guitar for Strangers With Candy," I say, imagining him missing notes, distracted by all those ankle-high breasts, and the woman lifts her index finger in the air, setting one of the broad-chested men into a walk-with-purpose stride toward us. STAFF, it says on his T-shirt, the letters three times the size of the lettering on Candy Girls' shirts but still not

1

spanning his chest. Over his shoulder I see my son step through the door behind the stage, and I wave.

The woman turns, and Aaron gives her a thumbs up. She shrugs like somebody learning from her television that another African country has declared itself free from the ruling military junta. "Okay," she says, dropping her hand. The security guard squints at me, but he turns back to the stage, mingling among the hundred or so fans, mostly male, who, though it's over an hour before Strangers With Candy are scheduled to start, are packing themselves together near the stage, drinking fast, smoking, jittery and bouncy. The two Candy Girls push their way through the men, each holding four bottles of Coors Light.

"It's getting crazy since the MTV thing," Aaron had said earlier in the week, "but I can get you into the dressing room before the show, and there's a place to watch from that's out of the crowd."

"What's crazy mean?" I'd said.

"You'll see."

"I listen to their CD 25 times a day and watch the MTV battle every day 5 times a day." – Crimson, a fan

The music my son's band plays attracts a mass celebration of controlled violence called moshing. It's not new. Neither is stage diving. Neither is crowd surfing. But now it is my son and his music driving the fans of Strangers With Candy to share this odd combination of joy and danger.

By the time Aaron finishes his sound check the crowd is twenty deep, packed to the sides of this club where a large banner proclaims COORS LIGHT WELCOMES MTV'S STRANGERS WITH CANDY. On a nearby sign, in smaller letters, is the warning NO MOSHING.

"The no moshing signs are bullshit," Aaron says five minutes later. "They're like no trespassing signs or no loitering signs. They make people do it. If the bouncers don't do their job, they don't mean anything, and this place looks like it doesn't have enough musclemen to take care of things."

I think of enormous barking dogs or occasional police rounds. I look around and see four huge men wearing STAFF shirts within twenty feet of us, and I remember Aaron's excitement the week before.

"The club had seven bouncers," Aaron had said when I'd called to ask how things had gone in New Jersey. "When we played there last month they had one." *MTV was better than yeast,* I'd thought. Strangers With Candy had won the title of MTV's Ultimate Cover Band three weeks before, and every place they played had suddenly swollen with fans. "The only thing that sucks," Aaron had said, "is that we'll have to change our name if we get signed. You know, Comedy Central started that stupid show with the same name."

"You have any ideas?" I'd asked.

"We're making a list. Right now, Driver is in first place."

Now I follow him up a short flight of stairs and into an abandoned kitchen that looks as if it could audition for *The Shining II.* There are huge, gleaming bowls haphazardly stacked on counters and the floor. Juice machines lie prone on countertops. There are cutting boards, sauce pans, and a griddle large enough to fry a small child on. Everything is strewn as if it had been arranged by the tumbling bodies of drunken fistfighters.

The door we go through next is unmarked. Behind it are a couple of old couches and a half dozen chairs. A counter holds two tubs of ice, one stocked with water bottles, the other with beer. Otherwise, the room is empty. "Pretty nice, huh?" Aaron says, and I shrug, gauging how stale the air is, thinking of my asthma, the inhaler in my pocket. He opens another door and we step into an old railroad car. "You can get through all that crap and check things out through a window," Aaron says. "You'll be right on top of us, but out of reach."

We turn back, and Aaron fishes Yuengling Lagers out of the ice for both of us. The rest of the band files in, and we shake hands. Chris, the drummer, has played with Aaron since they were in tenth grade. I had him in class at the university where I teach. I've met Mark, the bassist, and Nick, the singer, three times before. "This is Tony," Aaron says, and I shake hands with a twenty-two-year-old who calls himself DJ Worm and wears, even now, a ball cap with its bill angled, I'm sure, exactly where "cool and current" is located, somewhere between the ordinary of facing front and the worn-out hipness of reversed.

"Water or beer?" Nick says, standing between the ice buckets.

"Beer," Tony says. "Water makes me piss too much."

"You got a set list?" Nick asks Aaron.

"Let's do Korn first," Aaron says. "'Blind' and 'Falling Away from Me,' maybe some Rage, and then some of our shit."

"Oh my fucking God — where do I even start?
They are just flat out gorgeous." – Butterfly, a fan

4

I tell Aaron I want to stay in the crowd for a while. He rolls his eyes. "Go for it," he says. "As long as you know how to get to the safety zone. I'll see you later." On the club's floor a railing splits the long room in half, separating the bar area from the open pit that stretches back fifty feet from the stage. By now the crowd reaches nearly to the end of the bar. Up front, I count a dozen more Candy Girls by the stage. The woman at the door, as I work my way past her, shouts to one of the bouncers, "We're running out of wristbands." Just in front of the railing is a space that reminds me of an air pocket, and I slip into it, leaning against the railing to make sure nobody gets behind me. A minute later the stage lights go up, the spots running through red and blue and back again, everything flashing so rapidly Strangers With Candy looks as if it's arranging itself inside a pinball machine. Aaron machine guns the opening riff to "Blind," and the audience unanimously recognizes it and roars, surging forward, opening five feet of space in front of me as people pack closer to the stage. Aaron repeats the riff again and again, the crowd heaves, and then Nick takes the mike and growls, "Are you ready?" driving what looks to be fifty of the closest fans to bounce and then, a few seconds later, to slam into each other.

Not so bad, I say to myself. The space in front of me fills, but this far back the modest, early violence doesn't quite reach me. However, it's already so smoky I start to panic about my asthma, and I tell myself five more minutes and I'll work my way to that railroad car. "Blind" ends, and Aaron chimes the opening riff of "Falling Away from Me" as another hundred fans sweep around the railing into the surging crowd. "I want to see all you motherfuckers go crazy," Nick yells, and a few seconds later, when the song explodes, they do, the original fifty and a few dozen more just behind the two rows of Candy Girls slamming into each other, forearms and shoulders fending off other forearms and shoulders, a swirling pit that looks as if it could suck the crew of the *Pequod,* Ishmael included, through the club floor.

I walk past a bouncer who seems remarkably placid and go backstage. I lift a second beer from the ice bucket and begin to squeeze myself through hills of trash toward the front of the railroad car.

"There's a lot of shit in the way, so watch out," a voice I recognize says from near a window.

"Hey," I say, and I sidestep my way toward where Derek, my other son, is standing with Keri, his girlfriend. He's understating. Broken furniture. Unknowable metal fragments. Swaths of insulation. Old banners from previous shows: Bad Hair Day; 40 Lb. Head; UUU. I imagine the Strangers With Candy banner hanging above the heads of the crowd being shoved into the pile by a janitor. I imagine a COORS LIGHT WELCOMES DRIVER sign. I imagine myself tripping on the way back out and being impaled.

"We walked right by you," he says. "You were so into it I didn't have the heart to break the trance. Anyway, Aaron said he was going to put you up here. He knows what happens down there in the pit."

The window of the railroad car sits three feet above the heads of the craziest fans. Keri leans out, taking pictures with a camera I hope comes in a sturdy, crush-proof case. By now the mosh pit has become a tornado of chaos. It looks as if more than a hundred fans are slamming into each other, and I fix on one man whose eyes glitter unnaturally. He hurls himself against other bodies with ferocity. He punches the air so close to the faces of other moshers I nearly flinch. But I pick him because he's bleeding from a cut above his eye, blinking against the dripping even while he lunges toward the nearest group of frenzied fans as Nick screams a Rage Against the Machine chorus, "Lights out / Guerilla radio / Turn that shit up."

And then things settle a bit. The band plays its most melodic original and covers a long, complicated Tool song that keeps the moshing to a minimum. Forty minutes later, the last song of the first set is Filter's "Hey Man, Nice Shot." The crowd, knowing a break is imminent, launch themselves into a frenzy with each extended wail of the chorused title, but when I turn to my son and say, "It's not so bad," he grins.

"This is the wimpy set," he says.

"These guys mad rule." – Sparkle. a fan

The three of us work our way back to the lounge. Nick and Mark and Aaron change their sweat-soaked shirts. Chris opts to go shirtless. When Derek asks Nick to explain the set list strategy to me, he says, "We try to keep it just a little crazy for a while, but the second set is all the heaviest shit. They'll go fucking nuts."

"The bouncers get a workout," I say, and he laughs.

"Fuck, yeah," he says, helping himself to a beer, passing a bottle to everybody who's within arm's reach.

Sitting on the couch, the mosh-pit bleeder is getting attention, a girl in leather and leopard skin holding a compress to his eye. Aaron sees me staring. "This is Butch," he yells, waving me closer. "He's our professional fan."

We're introduced. Butch shrugs and shows me where he took stitches above the other eye a few weeks ago. "Three shows in three nights," he says. "There's bound to be damage, but fuck me, my fucking shirt's ruined."

He pulls up his blood-spattered black Strangers With Candy t-shirt. I wore mine when I watched the MTV show three Saturdays ago, drinking beer and eating nachos with Derek, Keri, my wife, and my friend Tom until the credits rolled up two hours after it began. Butch had worn his black shirt to the taping in New York's Roseland Ballroom. That night the Strangers With Candy version of "Guerilla Radio" had lasted forty-five seconds because of the format of the show, yet the camera had picked up a small, spontaneous mosh pit forming almost immediately. I think of going back to the tape I made and watching those moshers again, looking for Butch. Now, satisfied that the bleeding has stopped and the Band-aid is stable, Butch strips off the shirt and pulls on a red Strangers With Candy shirt. "I cut the band's hair," he says and laughs, pulling Nick under his arm. Their haircuts are nearly identical, jagged and short and a sort of glow-in-the-dark blond. Nick sports a new lip piercing, a tongue piercing, something shiny through his nose, but as far as I can tell, in the six weeks since I've last seen him, my son has restricted his piercings to multiple rings through his ears.

"This is John," my son says, and I shake hands with a beefy guy who has shaved his head to cue-ball slickness. He grins. "Aaron's Dad," he says, "good to fucking meet you." Though he's sweating and breathing heavy, he's not bleeding. "Butch is crazy," he says. "I try to exercise a little damage control out there. That's what comes from being a prison guard." He laughs again. "Lackawanna County Jail. You end up there, you look me up."

The people who wander into the room look my way, take in my age, the way I'm dressed, and then return to whatever they were doing. Their behavior tells me how non-threatening I look, so far out of line with anyone else I couldn't possibly be an undercover cop, so ordinarily dressed I couldn't be a record company executive.

Nick smiles when I tell him I remember him fronting a band when he was fifteen. "I was fourteen when I started," he says. "Those guys were in their forties."

"Like a Hanson brother playing with his father and his friends."

Nick laughs. "It was a fucking hair band," he says. "I had shit way down my back. Those guys were way too fucking old after a while." I go back to my beer. Those guys, like me, are in their fifties now.

A girl with pink hair is holding her side. "The pit's crazy tonight," she says. "The bouncers are sitting on their asses. Nobody's getting tossed."

She weighs, at most, 110. She's drunk, but so are five hundred other women in the club, and only a couple of dozen are in the pit.

"We can't get really hurt," she says. "It's like roller derby. You walk away with your shit still together."

Butch lifts her off the ground. "And we always stop to pick you up when you get your ass kicked."

She squirms and mock punches at him. "The mosh pit rules," she says. "You fall five hundred times a night, but the music's so fucking mad good you stop counting."

I settle into one of the couches, figuring the smoke for being less threatening closer to the floor, and a few seconds later three girls with astonishingly similar cleavage flop down beside me, throwing their heads back like pole dancers in a strip club. I consider the chances of my son getting one or more of these girls pregnant, but I skim past that worry to the possibilities of disease. I feel like asking each of them for one of those clean-health IDs some prostitutes carry like a union card. Suddenly, with thighs rubbing against me from either side, I'm turning as paranoid as any typecast father in a fifties juvenile delinquent movie.

Tony barely gets back to the band lounge before the last set is scheduled to start. He grins and launches a fast-talking story full of tight pants and large breasts. "I kept trying to walk away, but my dick kept talking."

"Those chicks are dumb," Nick says.

"They kept getting hotter every time they said something stupid."

"Dumb's not good enough," Aaron says. "They're real dumb."

Tony laughs. "You don't fuck their brains." He points at me. "Hey," he says, "you all seen his ride? Fucking tight. When you going to give me that?"

"If you can spell it, you can drive it home," Nick says.

Tony hesitates as if he's mulling it over. "I can spell *toy*," he says. "What the fuck is *ota?*"

I think of the university parking sticker on my new Celica parked two blocks from the club, how far Tony must have wandered in pursuing the hot, dumb chicks, how easily that car had turned his head. I realize I'm waiting for any one of the three girls on the couch to whimper even the smallest protest.

"Spell Tylenol," Butch tells him. "That and all the fucking beer we can swallow is what keeps us out there rocking." Tony doesn't change shirts. Twenty minutes outside in early March has chilled him down. One of the girls leans forward, flaps her top to create a breeze over her exposed breasts. She's so at ease with the motion I understand I'm the only one in the room who's aroused.

"These guys are the shit." – Syl, a fan

At the university, earlier in the week, I hosted a visiting writer, a poet. On the way to campus after dinner I slid the just-released Strangers With Candy CD in. Despite the fact that he is ten years younger than I am, it was so much like playing the music for my father that I turned the volume down. We were back to campus before one song ended. "If it wasn't your son playing, would you be listening to this?" he said.

I shrugged the way I do when the president of the university where I teach asks me, in passing, "How are things?" I've never said anything but "Okay" in twenty years, and it didn't please me then to acquiesce to politeness because he was a visiting writer, a peer, someone who writes poems and publishes in the same journals I do.

I knew what I'd do after his reading—slip in Rage Against the Machine or Tool and turn it up so loud I couldn't hear an ambulance if it was approaching my intersection from a ninety degree angle. The paper would say I was inexplicably broadsided; the autopsy would show no traces of drugs or alcohol in my system.

The truth is I've been driven to the loudest, most aggressive music since I started listening to rock and roll—Little Richard, James Brown, Blue Cheer, Iggy and the Stooges, Korn.

At school I can't say, "I want the music to kick ass." I'm educated, a professional, and every colleague I know talks about classical, jazz, or Broadway musicals. None of those genres fucking rules. None of them brings hysteria and chaos, thousands of people transfixed to physical risk. Truth be told, none of the literary writing that I and the visiting poet encourage in our workshop classes will be cranked up to jet-takeoff decibel level. Strangers With Candy is "mad good," not profound.

"I want to fuck Aaron's brains out." – Cindee. a fan

Nearly all the women I meet backstage have names like dolls: Tiffany, Kandee, Starr, Angel. Seemingly without exception, they smoke, and every one of them is thin. When I lean out of the railroad car window a few minutes after the second set begins I verify that smoking and thinness runs through the fifteen rows closest to the stage. Just behind them, the heavier women, most of whom don't light up, bloom here and there as if ChemLawn stopped spraying for weight thirty feet from the stage. A few rows later there's no distinction among fat and thin, smoker and nonsmoker, and I'm suddenly sure the names change to Sarah and Erica and Stacey.

By now the room looks as if it's gone beyond capacity. Derek and Keri move to the end of the window closest to the stage, and the woman in leather and leopard, standing just below us, yells up that the club ran out of wrist bands at one thousand, but let several hundred more people jam inside. It's past midnight, yet there's still a line filing past the woman checking IDs at the door. The mid-room railing looks vulnerable. I start to think of famous soccer crowds, fans crushed against restraining fences. The club seethes. It ripples from front to back and side to side. The pit swells to well over a hundred, and the rest bounce and pump their fists. I can find only those four bouncers, all of them by the stage, and none of them seems inclined to wade into the crowd. Their job, apparently, is to protect the band. Everybody else, for tonight, is on their own.

I recognize the opening riff of another Rage song. "Wah, wah, wuppa, wah, wah, wuppa wuppa, wuppa . . ." Aaron has enough foot pedals on his sound board to take his guitar from bells to jackhammers. Girls are passed across the top of the crowd. One in particular, Asian, wears a black tank top and pants that call up memories of the stylized stripes on Cincinnati Bengals' helmets. "How many times do you think she'll be groped?" Derek asks me, and I watch, beginning to count, comparing the numbers of hands on her breasts to those that find themselves high on her thighs.

"As many times as possible," I say.

The Candy Girls don't mosh, but while Butch slams and punches the air, other women throw themselves into the pit, slamming against the men, stumbling and falling. True to Butch's word, the moshers stop each time somebody falls. They lift the prone to their feet and then slam again.

"Bulls on parade," Nick repeats, his voice more hoarse each time over the relentless hook. By now every person in front of the mid-room railing is fist pumping and screaming along. I'm leaning far out of the window, mouthing the words, head bobbing until the song ends, and I say a *Fuck, yes* to myself, a great, silent orgasmic yelp that keeps me fixed on the sweaty shuddering of the nearest women.

Aaron launches the next opening riff, back-to-back Rage, this time "Know Your Enemy." Delivering the vocals, a fusion of rap and roar and melody, Nick looks as if he wants to skewer the complacent on his outthrust corkscrewing fist. I watch his feet, which seem to sense the last inch of stage he can occupy without tumbling into the turmoil of the pit, and then I concentrate on his staged anger, more convincing, despite his slight build and smooth face, than the theatrics of a professional wrestling villain. The women just below him look as if they'd welcome his hurtling body, ecstatic under the careening weight that would snap them down to the floor.

It's all I can do to notice my son, who's adopted a "look, no hands" sort of showmanship, running through the sound effects and lightning-fast fingerings as if he were strumming rhythm guitar in a folk band. He looks bemused, and the women below him gape with the astonishment of sex-charged school girls who would volunteer to be sawed in half by hands so deft.

"All of which are American dreams," Nick screams over and over, referring to *ignorance, brutality,* and *the elite,* among others, and then the song abruptly ends without me even seeing Chris or Mark or Tony.

Suddenly, Butch climbs on stage. Nick introduces him as their "craziest motherfucking fan," and when the band launches into its own song, "Idiot," Butch rocks back a step, then flings himself forward into the crowd.

"Fuck me, I'm fucked up anyway," Nick sings, "Everybody wants to change me," and the moshers fling themselves into the air, twirling and slamming forearms and shoulders into whoever is closest, roaring the lyrics. Butch is swept over the heads of the crowd followed by a girl modestly holding her blouse against her chest as she's flung, legs in the air, from the front to the back of the mosh pit.

One beefy guy, so sweat-soaked his hair sprays the moshers nearest him when he spins, forearms a woman to her knees. When he bends to help her up he's pushed on top of her in a way that takes the breath out of me. I lean forward, watching, and know I expect serious fondling, that I wouldn't be surprised if his hand ran up her thigh and wedged itself between her legs. And suddenly I understand that if I drifted off and stood by myself every gesture would turn as sordid as rough-sex pornography.

It slips away, this feeling. The woman, if she believed herself threatened, is laughing it off. "If you start to analyze, you'll have to leave," I hear Derek say. He passes me a beer as if it is penicillin for uneasiness.

Derek turns, and I follow his gaze to see two women working their way around the trash stacked on either side of the narrow path through the boxcar. Because they're both smoking, I rethink the old insulation and the paper, suddenly certain that a fire would surely kill us all. They climb onto the window ledge and scream at the nearest moshers. They're planning to dive into the crowd, but Keri, still holding her camera, taps one on the shoulder and points to where the wooden ledge is beginning to separate from the side of the car. "Fuck," the woman says. "Shit." She backs down and puts her feet on the floor, still leaning, and screams at the crowd again. Half-inch sections of four nails are visible, and her friend, when she finally turns her head, screws her cigarette into the ledge, drops it over the edge, and skids back into the car. "Fuck it," she says. "Thanks."

They disappear through the trash as "Idiot" ends, and a moment later I see the second woman come up behind Aaron and begin to climb the speaker stack beside him. It teeters a bit, but she manages to stand on the top, her feet level with Aaron's head. *Six feet plus three feet of stage,* I think, the speakers swaying as she pumps both fists.

"The roof, the roof, the roof is on fire," Nick begins to growl, and the bouncer underneath the speakers looks up like everyone else as the woman lifts her arms as Nick screams, "We don't need no water, let the motherfucker burn." She arcs into the crowd; a dozen hands reach up to catch her, then pass her overhead until she rolls sideways and drops to the floor as feet-first as any house cat.

A steady stream of stage divers follows, none of them chancing the speakers, thank God. The idea, after all, is to nearly get hurt, not to be crippled. You get talked about as a "crazy motherfucker." You get known among the faithful. You log onto the official Strangers With Candy web site with pen names like Full Metal Jacket and CandyCum and type in messages that proclaim how last night's show "kicked fucking ass" and you would "fuck you guys every day if at all possible."

At 1:20, knowing the last set is half over, I leave Derek and Keri in the window and make my way to where I'm almost back on the floor, standing at the shallow end of the ramp that leads to the old kitchen, keeping the railing between me and the crowd pressing near the stage.

The railing and the ramp fence off the crowd on my side, the rail-road car wall controls the other side, but every time the moshers heave forward, the Candy Girls and twenty other women sprawl from the waist up onto the stage, arms flailing over the monitors. And then they're up again, fist pumping, pogoing until they're hurled, caught at the thighs by the edge of the stage and folded forward.

A half hour of this—Deftones, more Korn—and then Nick announces they're finishing with three Strangers With Candy origi-nals. The crowd recognizes the first one, yelling out the lyrics—"You bore me, now what am I supposed to do?" When the song blows up in the middle, Aaron turning his guitar to chainsaw volume, they launch themselves into attack mode, bodies flying, women flailing to the floor, lifted, then falling again.

The second original calls up more sing-along—"Come to my room, to my bed," and then, when Nick bellows "What do you want?" the moshers slam against each other so ferociously three women and one man lurch to the floor almost simultaneously, the pit breaking into jagged, smaller groups, reforming, swirling, until, finally, at quar-ter to two, the moshers pause for maybe five seconds while Aaron cranks out the opening riff of "Heave."

Nick roars, "So, get the fuck up," and suddenly the mosh pit is so enormous it swells nearly to the bar, a couple hundred people caught up in what everybody knows is the last song. Bodies bounce off the railing in front of me. I watch a girl hurl herself, both feet off the floor, against two guys at the base of the ramp. She staggers back, then hurls herself again, screaming a second time, along with Nick, "So, get the fuck up."

There can't be more than five minutes of music left, but the smoke, down on the floor, is tightening my chest, so I go back up the ramp, through the empty kitchen, and I lift a beer from the huge ice bucket, nodding at a guy with his feet up on a couch. I slip into the deserted kitchen to listen from the relatively smoke-free zone. "Who the fuck are you?" I hear, and I turn to see that the stranger from the dressing room has followed me.

"Aaron's dad," I say, and he brightens.

"Really? Fucking great. I'm Chris." He extends his hand and tells me he's the brother of Corey, the band's new manager.

Part of the entourage, I think, and as soon as "Heave" ends we hear screaming from out front—"More. More. More."

"Fuck, yeah," Chris says, and the stage lights go dark.

"More. More. More," the crowd yells, and a moment later we hear the opening riff of "Break Stuff" and the stage lights go white as a Fourth-of-July sparkler. They snap on and off as Aaron repeats the riff. "Check it out from back in here," says Chris, and he leads me through a door that opens onto the back of the stage. We stand and watch, shadowed in that doorway. The girls in front are still leaning forward, pressing hard into the stage as if it was made of foam rubber. They throw their fists at the band, screaming the Limp Bizkit exhortation "break your fucking face tonight" as if they wanted to bring mayhem and harm to the owner of the nearest suspect expression, parting only when, the song ending, a tower of vodka shots is passed up to the band.

"They're going to get signed," Chris says. A roar goes up as all five band members tip their heads and drink.

"And turn into Driver," I say.

"Strangers. Driver. Whatever. They're off the hook," Chris says.

"There isn't a girl alive who wouldn't take candy from them."
– Sunshine. a fan

14

In the lounge I slump in a chair that has surely been in the room since rockabilly bands performed here. It takes less than a minute for me to disappear into the furniture as if I were Plastic Man, that old comic book character who transformed himself into any object. A group of girls who look as if they'd paid a group rate for fake IDs surround the band. One of them is having her red Strangers With Candy shirt signed.

"How dope are these guys?" one of the other girls says.

"They kick serious ass," another says. Both of them are wearing identically tight white pants and black tank tops. Both have short, cropped, neon-bright magenta hair.

The girl with the signed shirt twirls for the others. "How dope is that?" she says.

"That fucking rules," one of magenta twins says.

"I can't wait for the middie shirts to come in," the other says. "Wait until they sign that." I focus on her flat stomach, how it will look bared, the Strangers With Candy shirt cut so short the band will have to sign on the back or else scrawl across her breasts.

"These guys make Wilkes-Barre a cool place to live."

"Yeah, Pennsylvania isn't Bore State anymore."

Derek and his girlfriend are staying. Neither of them has asthma or fifty-four years to carry. I shake Aaron's hand and nod at the rest of the band. "You guys are good," I say, "real good," as close as I can get to "fucking rule," and then I duck through the stage entrance, fighting the urge to check who might be seeing me as someone made interesting by my access to the stage.

When I step outside, the first thing I hear is "Boring" blasting from the open window of a passing car. It's the first cut on the new CD. Two cars later, I hear "Boring" again, and I wonder how close those CD players are to being in sync, everything about this night so completely "mad good" I open the sun roof of my silver Celica and crank my copy of the CD. It's early March, but I can stand the cold for a few minutes. My ride is so fucking tight, I watch women as I roll slowly by them, imagining my age halved, getting laid through the double aphrodisiac of sleek car and kick-ass music.

Six blocks, and then nobody is walking. I roll shut the roof. The CD sounds even louder now, but there's such a ringing in my ears from the show I keep it cranked as if the noise can send my ambivalence into remission. I can listen to the CD three times before I get home. There are miles enough to nearly memorize each song before I crawl into bed at 3:30 and fall asleep to the shrill white noise of tinnitus.

Who's in the House?

"I Alone," Aaron says immediately, when I ask him the name of the first song Strangers With Candy played together.

In January 1999 Nick had driven to Selinsgrove from Berwick to try a new lineup for what was left of the band Breaking Benjamin. Ben, the band's singer and songwriter, had left for California in early December to see if he could shop his newest songs—songs that were softer and more Beatlesque than what Breaking Benjamin had been performing. Aaron was game. "Ben's gone," Aaron explained when Ben hadn't come back by Christmas. "He's into his own stuff out there."

Playing guitar in Breaking Benjamin had lasted only three months, just long enough for Aaron to get hooked on rehearsing and performing. Just long enough, in fact, to make him realize he wanted to play music as well as produce it, getting the most from his talent and the music engineering degree he had just received in Florida. He had joined the band when he came back home to live after finishing an internship at a music studio near Pittsburgh.

Getting together had been Hoover's idea. "Nick's a pro," he'd told Chris and Aaron. "He's into some heavy shit." Hoover was the bass player who would get fired six months later because, Aaron said then, "He just didn't get it that we were serious."

And neither did I at the time. I was relieved every time Breaking Benjamin actually was paid for playing. I was happy watching them, excited about how good I thought Ben's songs were, but that band, despite its promise, had fallen apart within months. So now I muted my enthusiasm about the new band, kept my responses to Aaron's reports about rehearsals to something that sounded very much like the "How was your day?" offered by the fathers in a thousand stories about benign neglect.

And when Aaron would say "Okay" and go upstairs to his room to practice during the nights he didn't go out as the assistant to Keith, a sound and light man who worked with bands in Central Pennsylvania, I would settle in front of the television or a stack of my students' short stories, the first two months of Strangers With Candy coming to me completely secondhand.

Their first public performance was in March. They were slated to play at Gooseberries, a little bar in Northumberland, eight miles from our house. Not really an official show at that, just an open mike night, but then there was a scheduling conflict, the open mike was closed, and the band, revved up and disgusted, declared they were playing back in Chris's basement for anybody who wanted to listen.

Derek had followed them. It turned out they were covering Weezer and Tool and enough other current bands to put on a show for ten friends who drank beer and cheered when each song ended. I shook my head as Derek told the story. An open mike had sounded to me like a euphemism for "unpaid amateur night." And this seemed even worse. "Chris's basement?" I said. "That's not promising."

"They just started, Dad," Derek insisted, saying it like the preface to a bad performance. "And Nick really got into it." I could tell he meant me to understand that it didn't matter if they stopped between songs to drink beer and talk, that it was more like friends in a college dorm room than a rock show. "When they cranked it up," Derek finally said, "Nick rocked."

Except for Derek the older brother and Nick the new singer, the rest of the guys in Chris's basement were old friends. With all the talk and pauses, the band filled over an hour for what might have passed for a poorly attended three-year high school reunion party. "'Play Motley Crüe,'" Derek quoted the drunkest of the twenty-one-year-olds. "He yelled it after every song," Derek went on. "I don't know what he was hearing, but I think he really believed they would do it if he kept shouting."

I nodded after each story Derek told. I didn't know anything more about the new band than the location of Chris's house, but Derek was sure they were declaring themselves ready for an audience.

"I was pissed the first time I saw them," Hyland says. We're sitting on the roof of his apartment in Wilkes-Barre, each of us holding a beer and watching a dozen sauce-slathered chicken parts searing on his grill. "Nobody told me Strangers With Candy was opening for Three Stoned Men, and I was the manager." Hyland smiles. "I hadn't heard them play yet, but I saw their set list and thought they had balls, playing stuff that nobody else played. You know, like 'Stuck.' I knew that was hard to play, but they did Bizkit better than Bizkit. And their Deftones stuff was the shit. After I listened, I wanted to represent them too."

He's telling me about the band's first "real" show. "April Fool's Day," he says. "There's an omen or something." He laughs, comfortable with how good Strangers With Candy is. I'm glad he feels that way, but sitting here in the middle of the summer, I remember seeing the band for the first time a month after they impressed Hyland and six weeks after Gooseberries and not sharing that opinion.

Strangers With Candy was still getting nearly all of their gigs by opening for Three Stoned Men, a band that covered similar rap metal and alternative groups, and on this night in early May, Three Stoned Men had been hired to warm up the crowd entering Tink's, a Scranton club, to hear Fuel, a national act, which had an opening band of its own. The mathematics of where Strangers With Candy crouched in this hierarchy of recognition was discouraging—opening for a band that wasn't even an opening band. The only people more distant from the real show were my wife and me, who had driven a hundred miles to see, for the first time, our son's new band play in front of an audience.

After he spent two minutes hyping his radio station and the free pizza being passed around by interns, a deejay who called himself Sausage introduced Strangers With Candy. (Just over a year later, inside Tink's, Sausage would extend his introduction of the band for as long as possible, stringing together superlatives until he reached the crescendo: "And now, Universal/Republic recording artists—Strangers With Candy.")

Perhaps twenty people were paying attention. The line had begun to form to get inside for a show by a band that had two hit singles already, and I noticed that most of those patrons were talking among themselves and facing away from Strangers With Candy. During the first two songs I kept my eyes open for turned heads and dancing feet, but none of the passers-by, many of them exiting the municipal building behind the band, did anything but locate their cars and drive off into the early evening.

Finally, two girls and one guy began dancing in the street. He was the most agile of the three, jumping and spinning, but he seemed to be hearing something other than the songs Strangers With Candy was playing. Nearby, though, a trio of street people were closer to the rhythm. A squat black woman who looked both retarded and drunk pitched back and forth, laughing with pleasure.

The police watched from behind the band, but they didn't seem to be on duty. The station where they were headquartered was a few steps away. There weren't enough people to demand security.

A woman was filming the show with a video camera. "That's Nick's mom, I think," my wife said, and I asked her how she knew this. "Aaron told us she comes to every show and videotapes them all," Liz said, and I glanced at the woman again, remembering only that Aaron had said, "Nick's mom is way younger than you guys."

The street show was one forty-minute set. That worked out to ten songs, but after seven Sausage leaned close to Nick, and the next thing we heard was "We have two more for you," meaning that the secret message Nick had heard was an order to cut one song to stay within the time limit. Fortunately, they hadn't been asked to add half an hour to their show, because they only knew fifteen songs, what they needed to play their regular one-hour opening set.

The woman who had to be Nick's mother moved directly in front of us to film, and there was no question Aaron was right about her. She looked at least ten years younger than my wife, and I knew Nick, at twenty-three, was a year older than Aaron.

The street people stayed into the music to the very end. Two of them danced and strutted while the other one, a man so old I wondered how he managed the Scranton winters, watched and grinned. If they crossed the street, I thought, they could extend their hands for the free pizza and Pepsi before those radio station interns took the rock station's promotion inside where the action was migrating.

As I watched, I thought Aaron had taken a musical step backwards. Six months earlier he had been in Breaking Benjamin, a band with more than a dozen strong originals, yet here, on the street, Strangers With Candy played seven covers and two originals, one of them a Breaking Benjamin song "given" to them by Ben. I remembered how professional Breaking Benjamin had sounded. They'd opened for Cypress Hill at Susquehanna University, where I teach, and I had a tape of that performance in my car, a video of it on the shelf beside my television. Everything about that show had been better than what I was seeing and hearing except for the fact that now my son was relaxed and sure of himself. He was the only guitarist in this band; he was an equal partner in forming this group, not someone who had joined it after all the other members had played together for months. And Nick, who must have been born when his mother was still in her teens, had enough charisma to make up for the occasional ragged edge.

Aaron told me the next day that after we left the bouncers wouldn't let Strangers With Candy in to see Fuel. "We did the warm-up show in the street, and then this ID Nazi told us we can't get in."

"You mean without a ticket?" I asked.

"Exactly. That's not ever part of the discussion," Aaron said. "But at least the guys from Fuel checked us out while we were playing. That was cool, except Hoover brought up the Cypress Hill gig to them. That doesn't get said. Hoover doesn't get it."

"You're playing at Knockers?" I asked a week after their street performance, and Aaron shrugged.

"It hasn't been Knockers for months, Dad," he said. "It's called Studio 15 now."

"It will always be Knockers," I said, remembering the busty, cleavage-showing woman being pursued by a wolf that passed for a logo for the local cover-version of Hooters.

"What does a place like Knockers pay?"

Aaron frowned. "The first time is free," he said. "It's like an audition. If they decide to have us back we get $150."

"How many bands get a second date?"

"I know," he said. "It sucks."

Though Studio 15 is only two miles from my house, I thought of the empty Scranton street and, worse, the clouds of cigarette smoke that would surely aggravate my asthma. I shouldn't have worried. The next day Aaron told me that the total crowd, including Derek and the friend who went with him, was eight.

"Eight," Aaron repeated. "And you know what? Even when I was just unpacking my stuff before the show these two guys started hassling us. 'Come on,' they kept saying. 'We're waiting.' They all looked like truckers or something, guys staying at the motel out back. And then Hoover got in their faces."

I tried to picture the impatient truckers; I worked on imagining "in their faces" with Hoover as point man. "He told them to back off. He's always ready for something. He's a karate dude."

"I bet that helped," I said.

Aaron gave me a hopeless shoulder shrug. "'You guys suck,' one of them kept saying. We hadn't played a note. 'You guys suck.' What the hell? They were on coke or something. All wired up and jittery. I thought if I even made eye contact there'd be a fight."

"Trust me, Dad," Derek said, "it was worse than that. 'You fucking suck, you fucking suck, you fucking suck'—they just kept it up like a football cheer. And then it was 'Start playing now, start playing now, start playing now'—a couple of dumbasses on some kind of uppers."

Aaron shrugged as if he was trying to shed a coat of many disappointments, and so I knew Derek's recounting was accurate. "They shouted for Rage, and when 'Guerilla Radio' started, they did a stupid dance to make fun of the band. You know, like it was a pop song, an 'N Sync kind of thing. Nothing was stopping them."

"Not even Hoover?" I said, unable to imagine Aaron in any sort of fight.

"They had another chant after Hoover spoke up," Derek said. "'We never lose, we never lose, we never lose.'"

"That's why Hyland represents us now," Aaron finally said. "We need somebody to sort out the shit so we don't have to deal with that."

Derek nodded. "Totally unacceptable," he said. "Nobody goes in there ever again."

My sense of Strangers With Candy's early progress comes more from Derek than it does from Aaron, whose descriptions usually go something like "It was cool" or "It kind of sucked," those succinct reviews pegged, I know, to the size of the crowd.

"They're playing to dozens," Derek says. "That's what an opening band does."

Shortly after I see them play the street show, Derek convinces his sister, Shannon, and her fiancé, David, to make the trip from New York City to northeast Pennsylvania for a show. This one, he tells them, is at "a club just outside Wilkes-Barre," which means that all of them get lost trying to find a rural bar. And worse, because the crowd, when the show begins, is the three of them and four guys who look like they're waiting for Lynrd Skynrd's comeback tour, there's near silence between songs throughout the first set.

"Hard core hicks," Derek says, "and when the first set ended, these guys asked if they could play during the break."

"Uh-oh," I say, because there's no point in asking whether or not they did.

"So these three drunk dudes go on stage to play for their buddy and the bartender, using the band's equipment. It was all old heavy stuff—Iron Maiden, Ozzy—you know what I'm talking about. I don't know what Aaron and those guys were thinking."

A funny story, maybe, since Derek says nothing about Aaron's guitar being broken or Chris's drums being damaged, but he's not through. "It was later when it got ugly," he says. "Some jackass had a stun gun and was waving it around. By then there were people, enough to make it crowded in a small-ass place like that out in the sticks."

I think cattle prod. Stockyards. Riot control. And since Derek is volunteering this, I ask, "Who got zapped?"

"Nobody," Derek says, but before I can settle into relief, he goes on. "But he started waving it near Shannon, and she told him to knock it off, and that got him going. He was fucking with her, acting like he was going to use it on her, and it got crazy. You know Shannon. She's giving this guy shit, and he's all drunk. It was tense for a while."

"So why is this guy not thrown out?"

"It turns out he's the cook. He works there. A place like this doesn't have security, Dad. We're talking hick bar. It was up to us."

Aaron, when I ask him the next day, picks up the story when it reaches his eyewitness end of it outside the bar. "That drunk dude came out after the show when we were loading out. Some of our stuff was on the ground near the van, and he pissed on it."

"What?" I begin, and Aaron becomes more exact.

"Not right on it," he says, "but right beside it, so our stuff was being sprayed like it was maybe an accident or maybe on purpose. You know. He was fucking with us. Hoover really got jacked up. I was nervous. Hoover keeps a gun in his duffel bag."

"Why?" I ask, the question applying to any one of the details of Aaron's story.

"I shouldn't have said anything," Aaron says at once. "It's okay. It's all part of the life."

And despite every instinct I have as a father, I nod like a first-day teacher accepting gum chewing, smoking, and hidden weapons as things that are commonplace in high school.

In late June Strangers With Candy hires a new bass player. Mark plays with the George Wesley Band, a reggae group, and says he is waiting a few weeks to see how things work out, but for now he looks like he's going to stick. "We can finally go fast," Aaron tells me. "He can help write songs. He gives a damn about being good."

The downside is somebody has to tell Hoover he's fired, which doesn't happen until after the new lineup has already done a photo shoot for upcoming P.R. "We're thinking of going with Media Five," Aaron says. "They're the biggest booking agent around here. They handled Fuel and Live. Hyland's been cool and all, but we have to think bigger."

I think of Hyland and his enthusiasm. I think of Hoover and how he organized this band. Already there is a small litter of casualties, but Aaron is happier when he comes home from rehearsals now, and so, therefore, am I. He has only two moods about Strangers With Candy. He either thinks they'll be huge or is absolutely certain nobody cares. For now, the fresh lineup brings a high spike of optimism. The Media Five decision isn't final, but it feels like it's been made.

In early July Derek carries a tape into the house and pops it into the VCR. "Watch," he says, and I do. Transformed is what the band is. A bass player, so anonymous to me, suddenly liberates Aaron and Nick to perform with confidence.

It's wonderful to hear and see the improvement, but after I watch the videotape through three songs I have to say, "Where is everybody?"

"There's people there," Derek says, "you just can't see them."

"Where are you?"

"In the back where I always am. These places aren't that big."

During the fourth song somebody walks up near the stage and starts taking pictures. "Finally," I say.

Derek laughs. "That's Shannon," he says. "Your daughter."

"She's wearing a floppy hat," I say. "Everybody looks the same when they wear floppy hats." I could keep arguing, but what I'm thinking is the place is so deserted she's free to take close-ups of everybody, including Chris, if she has a mind to climb onstage and stand beside his drum kit.

I'm relieved that when they finish the first set I can hear a few whoops of approval, a scattering of applause. What I also understand is they still don't know enough songs to fill out a two-hour gig, because Nick comes back with a guitar to play a solo set, standing still and strumming, singing REM and the Beatles as if nobody would remember he'd just finished covering Rage Against the Machine.

And when he walks off and the others return it's Aaron's turn to pad the show, running through an instrumental, Dick Dale's "Miserlou," the old reverb surf classic revived for *Pulp Fiction*. I love this song, have a copy on a shelf within three steps of where I'm sitting, but it's as if Aaron has been cloned into a replica of himself who's in love with the early 60s, his real body standing backstage waiting for Nick to scream "Get the fuck up" before he'll replace this substitute guitarist. The rest of whatever crowd Derek insists is there is waiting as well. In front of the stage remains a space open enough for a pickup game of basketball. Farther back is the small, shy, mysterious audience.

It had been my idea to have Strangers With Candy play for an audience of teenagers attending a university-sponsored writers' camp. "I can give you $300," I'd said to Aaron in April, a time when that figure seemed generous, the idea of a manager was new to them, and I'd never seen Strangers With Candy play.

By July, with Hyland's help, they are sometimes playing for twice that, but Aaron's promise is kept. What made it easier is the fact that I'd scheduled them for Wednesday night, a time, Aaron admits, they're less likely to be busy. "Ninety minutes," I say, "sounds about right," and Aaron shrugs.

"We know enough songs to keep your kids there all night," he says.

I have sixty-five students, fifty-five of them girls, on campus for a week of fiction and poetry and screenwriting workshops. The business school has about thirty, mostly boys, and they chip in $100 to have their campers attend. It's a small bonanza for my budget, but Aaron, the day of the show, points out that Keith, the light and sound guy they need, gets $150 regardless. "Maybe I can work him down to $100 because I still go out on jobs with him, but I doubt it," Aaron says.

I don't want to do the math, but I can't help myself: $150 divided by four is $37.50 per band member for nearly five hours of their time if I include travel. Pizza delivery, which Aaron still does two nights a week, pays that well, and audience reaction to pizza, if it's downbeat, happens after he is safely down the highway. The Media Five signing looks certain, but Hyland is already successfully hyping them as head-liners. Three days from now they have a headline gig, $400, the PA system supplied by the club; next week they have a $600 date.

Chris and Aaron know the Susquehanna cafeteria. They played there the October before, when Breaking Benjamin won the Susquehanna University Battle of the Bands and received $300 they didn't have to split with a sound and light man. Chris was a senior then, making them eligible as a student group. Aaron claimed his father as a full-time employee to give them more credibility as a Susquehanna band. Hoover, on the application form, said he had signed up for a course once—true enough, though he'd never attend-ed a class.

The cafeteria, according to my students, looks like an airplane hanger, and after nearly all the tables have been cleared to the side and back, it's an undeniably accurate simile. With less than a hundred students inside, nearly all of them taking seats farthest from the tem-porary stage, it's cavernous enough to welcome a couple of Piper Cubs and one of those commuter planes that terrify me when it banks and lets me look straight down at the dwindling runway.

Mark, the new bassist, shakes my hand immediately, happy, he says, to meet Aaron's dad. He looks fierce—his head is shaved, and he's wearing a wifebeater that exposes what I sense is just the begin-ning of a tattoo collection on his arms. In fact, everybody is relaxed but me, because I can tell a dozen of my students have opted not to come. "I never heard of them," a girl had whined when I'd announced the event on Sunday night. "Your son's band?" somebody else had said, her tone suggesting her suspicions about Dad staging an ama-teur night.

"So what do you think?" I ask Chris. "This make you want to come back to school?"

"Not much," he says.

"You can write a sequel to your paper about Seed," I go on, bring-ing up freshman writing seminar, the class he endured with me as instructor every Tuesday and Thursday morning at 8 A.M. during his first semester.

Chris smiles. "That was the best thing I ever wrote. You told us to write about something that matters to us."

Chris and Aaron had been in a band called Seed during their sophomore and junior years in high school. They'd played for earlier versions of this writers' camp two years in a row when they were the same age as the campers, who loved their covers of Pearl Jam and Stone Temple Pilots, even squealing after each of the four originals the band had recorded at a studio in Lebanon, a place, seventy miles away, that my wife and I had to drive them to because not one of them was sixteen years old. During those two summer camp nights they'd sold, for five dollars each, a couple dozen of the tapes they had manufactured.

"What's happening out there?" Nick says as a sonic blast erupts from Aaron's guitar. "We're Strangers With Candy."

After two songs the business students exit in a group, and ten of mine drift into the shadows near the side door, using the area as a halfway house toward an evening elsewhere. Derek arrives. "See how tight they are?" he says as soon as an old Jane's Addiction song ends, and I nod unconvincingly, keeping an eye on the rest of my campers.

The band plays Deftones, Limp Bizkit, and Tool. Ten more students funnel through the side door, but the thirty who stay move up front. They jump and scream and playfully mosh. They hear Red Hot Chili Peppers, 311, Weezer. In the middle of the eighteen covers is "My Room," Strangers With Candy's one genuine original. Nick raps furiously until the song slows to allow him to moan plaintively, cajoling the high school girls who stand arm's length away to "come to my room, to my bed."

"Which one's your son?" one of the girls rushes over to ask me.

"The guitarist."

She turns toward the stage, then back again, smiling. "He's hot."

I look at Aaron, who's wearing a bowling shirt and dark-rimmed glasses. *Hot* doesn't occur to me, but this second look at them has me revved and bouncing in place. There's no question these guys are a band now. And Aaron plays with such assurance it's a joy to watch him.

The music thunders from the cafeteria and down the hall of the campus center to where the Security Office is located. At exactly 10 P.M., when the time I've reserved expires, a woman in a maroon shirt bearing the Susquehanna logo steps through the door and flips the switches for every bank of light in the cafeteria. The students and the band squint as if they're facing, from the back seat of a heaving car, the huge flashlight of a midnight park patrolman. She disappears and is replaced by a campus security officer, who stands in the doorway, arms folded across his chest, until the song ends. "Well," Nick says from the stage, "I guess the show's over."

Ten minutes later, the security officer confides to me in the hall, "I liked them better when they were that other band."

"You mean Breaking Benjamin?"

"That's it. They were good. I remember liking them when they won that contest." He shakes his head as if he expects me to begin a lament about the lousy choices our sons make.

Near midnight, Nick walks into the house with Aaron. So much a presence while he's rapping and roaring and singing, he's short and slight and nearly reticent offstage. "This is a really nice house," he says, standing in the living room, looking out our oversized windows toward the university a half mile away.

Aaron paces in the kitchen, ready for a few hours of unwinding. "I tried to keep my language under control," Nick says before he leaves. "I hardly ever said 'fuck.' I didn't want to get you in trouble."

"I say 'fuck' sometimes," I say, and he laughs.

Hyland, when he starts telling stories about the earliest of Strangers With Candy's shows, becomes animated. There's no question he's in love with this world. Even when Chris and Mark and my son slouch into chairs on the roof of Hyland's apartment, that barbecued chicken nearly ready, he launches into a new story about The Trillo, a nearby club managed by the son of the man who owns it. "There was a fuck-up," Hyland says. "They each booked a different act for the same night, and one of them was Strangers."

Chris and Aaron laugh, a sign that this is a story worth hearing. Mark, who wasn't in the band when they played The Trillo, smiles like somebody who's heard this story second hand. "Mere Mortals," Hyland says. "That was the name of the other act. Major fuck-up for crowd response. That band has acoustic guitars in it."

"There was only half a crowd anyway," Aaron says, poking at the chicken, but Hyland is rolling now.

"The club decided to have the bands do alternate sets. Can you imagine? Guys that play acoustic waiting while Strangers does Rage and Tool. The fucking manager, the son, he starts making slashing motions to his throat after two songs. What the hell. I'm not his father double-booking Strangers. But after four songs I pulled the guys off the stage, and that's when the shit started."

Chris rips open a bag of tortilla chips and unscrews the cap from a jar of salsa. "Nick threw down the mike," he says, "and started going off on the place. You know, 'This place sucks. Fuck this place.' All that kind of shit."

"Nick was Nick," Hyland agrees. "It wasn't a good moment."

"One less place for us to play in northeast Pennsylvania," Aaron says.

Hyland reaches for all our empty bottles. "But you got paid," he says, before he disappears down the stairs to get everybody another round.

While he's gone, Aaron lifts the chicken from the grill onto a plate. "We shouldn't even have been invited back that time," he offers. "We were there before that, and Nick pissed in the corner of the band room they were having remodeled. Just like that, for no reason. And Hoover punched his fist through the wall and smeared his blood everywhere."

"I haven't heard this one," Mark says.

"It's one to put behind us," Aaron says. "We were opening for Three Stoned Men back then, and they got blamed. The double booking was worse. We had to load out in front of the crowd when Hyland pulled us off. That was weak. The bouncers got in our face the whole time."

I nod. Chris and Aaron are still commuting to Wilkes-Barre from Selinsgrove. They're both working for Gelnett, a company that installs sound systems or provides and monitors them for special occasions. Aaron had worked graduation at Susquehanna; he'd miked the Board of Directors meeting where part of the discussion had been about the writing program I direct. I have no idea what Mark and Nick do to pay their bills, but the advice I think of at that moment is to be good to club owners so you're asked back.

Hyland reappears with fresh beer all around. For somebody who knows he's being phased out as manager, he's in remarkable spirits. "I know these guys are going to tear shit up," he's told me. "I know what they need to do to get their shit straight."

In August I ask Aaron if he has copies of the CDs that contain the songs they cover. "Sure," he says, and I make a tape of the parts of their show I like best: Rage Against the Machine, Tool, Limp Bizkit.

"Why don't you do Korn?" I say.

"Korn's tricky, so we haven't done much yet." Aaron smiles. "This stuff isn't all the same, Dad. But we'll have them nailed pretty soon."

He tells me the owners are closing Jitterbug's, the club where they've become regulars, first as an opening act, and lately as headliners. "What bad timing," I say, and he nods.

"It was a steady gig, all right, but there's one last show," he says. "Everybody's playing."

"Everybody?"

"Yeah, and we're next to last, going on at midnight. Only Cider's after us, and they've been around forever.

"We finally told Hyland we have to fire him. He's cool with it. He knows it's time for us to move on."

I think of the pile of chicken drumsticks I scarfed on Hyland's roof, his joy as he talked about Strangers With Candy. "Cool with it" sounds like nothing I could be but somehow accurate for Hyland, who apparently wasn't lying to me a week earlier.

"We're going to sign on with Media Five. Remember I told you about them? As soon as Mark made a commitment we had that photo shoot so we'd be ready to move. Media Five's the biggest thing around here. It's more than just they've done Fuel and Live. They'll get us all over New Jersey."

I understand he's telling me their status has risen in Wilkes-Barre and Scranton, that playing two sets later than Three Stoned Men means they've blown by the band that gave them a start by letting them open for them in April and May and June.

Jitterbug's, a week later, is packed by the time a band called Emily's Toybox finishes and Strangers With Candy begins to set up. When the band walks off, satisfied with their hasty sound check, Alan and Tom, two local entertainment writers, banter with each other while the crowd grows restless. I remember that Alan has been skeptical about Strangers With Candy, that he must be doing this out of obligation rather than enthusiasm. "My mother always told me to never fucking take candy from strangers," Tom says into the microphone. "But please," Alan responds, "welcome Strangers With Candy."

I give myself up to it all, leaning forward as the house lights go off in the first genuine rock-club venue I've ever been in, and a recording of the Oompa Loompa song from *Willy Wonka and the Chocolate Factory* reaches through the darkness: "What do you get when you guzzle down sweets? / Eating as much as an elephant eats?" And then, my son and the rest of Strangers With Candy materialize inside roiling, back-lit, crimson-colored fog. I push myself between two pairs of bare-midriffed women and squint as if I am peering into the artificial night for signs of the axe-wielding Jason Voorhees just as Aaron rips into the opening riff of "Break Stuff," the lights coming up strobe-brilliant when Nick, dressed in a white mental-hospital jumpsuit, tears into the lyrics. The crowd seems tentative, waiting to see whether Strangers With Candy demands full attention. Before the song ends, Nick's jumpsuit rips open, threatening to collapse around his ankles. "My fucking pants are falling off," Nick ad-libs, knotting the loose ends around his waist, cinching in his black tank top. He roars on. The band has swagger now, stage presence. A few hands are raised overhead throughout the crowd. Small clusters of bodies, including the two women to my right, jump in place, their cut-off shirts lifting achingly high.

A man wearing a T-shirt that reads MY DICK SMELLS LIKE CHAP-STICK lifts a beer in salute. I try to work out the sexual implications of that declaration, but when he turns around I see that the front of the shirt has a logo for Emily's Toybox, the band that preceded Strangers With Candy. I work to remember their music, but every tune has already slipped away, leaving behind just that T-shirt statement.

Between songs Nick cajoles the crowd, enticing them down front. "We want to see you all go fucking crazy, and we're not going to stop until you do," he says. Hands are raised overhead throughout all of the crowd now. Bodies are jumping in place, shoulders slamming off nearby shoulders. "Jump Around," Nick sings. "Jump up, jump up, and get down."

Five minutes later, the club going beyond unbearably hot, Nick pauses, standing in front of the large banner that repeats, four times over, the logo of The Bear, 97.9 & 95.7, Northeast PA's Rock Station. "You guys are all standing still," Nick says. "What's going on?" And then there are whoops and screams because Aaron is running through the intro of "Know Your Enemy." Nick seems to perk up. "All right, you fuckers," he roars, "you know what to do."

This time there's a sustained cheer at the end. Aaron changes into his Superman T-shirt, takes off his fake glasses as if Clark Kent himself had left the building, and begins the rapid-fire intro to their heavy cover version of the old Ah-Ha song "Take On Me." A mosh pit develops, small but crazy. Another Limp Bizkit cover follows, and when Nick yells, "Get your ass up," the first six rows of fans all do, making me feel that I've turned to stone. When a woman is lifted onto sets of raised hands, the men nearest to me murmur, "Fuck, yes," as if her flailing body certifies success. They push toward her, lifting their arms like disciples, and I step back, as suddenly self-conscious as a high-schooler fumbling a fake ID from his wallet at the liquor store.

"We'd like to play a couple of our songs now," Nick says. "Cider will be out in a little while. They kick fucking ass."

I hold my breath. Except for the street-thin and cafeteria-muffled versions of "My Room," I've never heard anything they've written. "Heave" begins with a relentless but muted riff, but it builds until Aaron rides the pre-hook and Nick screams, "So, get the fuck up" and, to my joy, the crowd does, a full-scale mosh pit forming, another female fan thrust above the crowd and carried along overhead. And when, halfway through "Key of Me," the second original, Nick crouches down in a cloud of stage smoke, moaning, "Your eyes are closed, but you can see that you're a fool." he gives it the full histrionic treatment, rising as the song steams into his full-throated, sustained moan just before it explodes into its hook. I'm sold. I start to look around and gauge the reaction of the crowd.

A guy behind me leans toward his friend. "They're smoking, aren't they?"

"Fucking hot."

"The originals are real good."

"Real good."

"I told you."

"I can have fun with this band."

And there it is, I think, turning back to the stage as Limp Bizkit's "Nookie" begins, everybody bouncing because it's all over the radio. And then, to close their set, they do "My Room," clearer now, more assured. "Last time at Jitterbug's," Nick drops into his rap, and the place goes nuts.

"We're huge," Aaron says, ecstatic afterwards, meaning it, at least until the next time only thirty people show up and all of them stand and stare. "This is going nowhere," he'll say then, meaning that, too, until another large crowd goes crazy. It's August, five months into the public life of Strangers With Candy, and they're going to play in New Jersey and Allentown throughout September, beginning to be booked regionally by Media Five. "I'm done delivering pizzas," Aaron announces. "If this takes off, I'm going to quit Gelnett, too, at the end of September, and move."

The whole band is animated. They're headliner material, and they seem to know it, the band in the all-night lineup that gets the buzz. Aaron is triumphant. The Bear, he tells me, is going to start playing a live version of "My Room."

"Freddie's into us," Aaron says. "He's the best DJ on The Bear."

A week later, riding home on a Sunday evening from visiting our daughter in New York City, my wife and I try to tune in to The Bear as soon as we cross back into Pennsylvania. Sunday night, Aaron had said, was when they played local music.

For ten miles the Spanish radio station from New York won't give up. We hear the faint overlap of heavy rock, but the Salsa tunes keep drifting back in, the announcer spewing Spanish so fast my wife, the former Spanish major, can't follow. By now it's 8:15. The show starts at 8:00. And then it's 8:30, the Spanish and English equally fading in and out before, at last, The Bear takes over for good and we're attentive to songs we'd ordinarily turn off, letting the station play on like my father would, setting his radio to KDKA in Pittsburgh for life.

By 9:00 we're speeding through the Poconos. By 9:15 we're nearing the intersection with the highway that drives fifteen miles north to Wilkes-Barre. "Maybe we missed it," I say.

"Maybe they're not playing it," my wife says.

And then, at 9:35, when we're halfway between Wilkes-Barre and Selinsgrove, Strangers With Candy comes on, and I turn it up, the song jumping out of the radio, even this muddy, live recording sounding fresh.

A minute after they're finished I shut off the radio even though we're still forty minutes from home. I recognize this scene from a dozen movies about musicians driving in their cars and hearing their songs for the first time, how the radio transforms the music, how it seems real now, permanent somehow because an enormous audience scattered over a fifty-mile radius is simultaneously receiving your song.

It's a hackneyed "moment of arrival," but it's thrilling nonetheless.

Get Crazy Out There

Late in the summer, I take an opportunity to see Strangers With Candy play earlier than midnight, for once, at something called Wilapalooza.

"An all-day festival. It's in Wila," Aaron says, leaving the rest for me to extrapolate. I've lived within thirty miles of Wila for twenty years and have never heard of it, but it's on the way to Harrisburg, and it would help the band immensely to get a following in another city besides the ones in which they've played most of their shows— Wilkes-Barre, Scranton, Hazleton, and Allentown.

"They're even tighter now," Derek says. "You'll see." He's gone to fifteen shows already, five of them in the two weeks since the last one I saw, and he's decided to ride along with my wife and me. "Bring my summer average up to three times a week," he says, unfolding the hand-drawn map Aaron has left for us.

The show, nine fifty-minute sets beginning at noon, is outdoors, a selling point for my bronchial tubes. Strangers With Candy is supposed to play around 8 P.M., two groups from the end. It sounds like a middle-aged man's idea of a sensible performance, and we go early, arrive before 6 P.M., because, I hazard aloud as we drive, "Why not see a couple of other acts, maybe stay for the one after?"

"And there's no way they won't have a beer tent," Derek says.

"Why not have a couple of beers and relax in the summer twilight?" I say to my wife, and she grimaces.

"Just what you need," Liz says, and she stares at the map as if it has an X for the site of Blackbeard's treasure.

Derek laughs. "Dad will go crazy. He'll bounce in place. You can check to see if his feet leave the ground."

The location is so rural, the directions so convoluted, I'm convinced, during each of the last fifteen minutes of the ride, that despite the map we've missed a crucial turn. The road leading to Yasgur's Farm is a freeway compared to the winding, crushed-stone lane leading to the site; old Max Yasgur himself might think himself too far out in the sticks walking down the hillside toward the stage where a group called The Martini Brothers is halfway through its set as we finally, after three final, worrisome turns, arrive.

"Twenty years we've lived here and neither of us has ever heard of Wila," I say, settling in a hundred feet from the stage. "How can that be?"

My wife shakes her head. "Because it's the middle of nowhere," she says. She's still holding the hand-drawn map Aaron gave us. "We'll have to use this going home. And it will be dark."

"Elk Road," I say. "A left instead of a right going backwards, two miles to Sand and another left. I'll need you to see the signs in the dark, not to be looking at that piece of paper."

I squint, the late afternoon sun in my eyes. "There wasn't even a sign for this," my wife says. "What's Wilapalooza anyway? There's hardly anybody here."

The Martini Brothers are well-known in the Harrisburg area, headliners among the nine bands at this festival, so I'm sure they're playing mid-program because they have an evening show to do somewhere else, that they need to get this set over with and be on their way. They play amplified rockabilly, complete with 50s outfits. They're professional and a pleasure to listen to, but the crowd is sparse, a couple hundred people scattered over the hillside, an equal number beginning to congregate near the beer and food behind the stage. Four songs later they leave their equipment for two roadies to deal with and ride off, to the admiration of a hundred redneck-looking beer swillers on large Harleys.

Twenty minutes later an area band that plays mostly covers of 80s music goes on. They churn out familiar songs by past hit makers like Tommy Tutone and Flock of Seagulls, the pop music you'd be nostalgic for if you graduated from high school in 1983, but nobody in the crowd, not even near the stage, is even bouncing in place. The drummer, heavy and sweating, manages to chain smoke through the set, lighting up, I notice, after every other song. The vocals are somewhere around adequate, I offer, though Derek says, "You're being kind, Dad. There's no need for that."

"Okay," I say, "they're awful."

My wife, ever cautious, tells me to lower my voice. "You never know," she says, "who might be sitting next to you at something like this." I look around, considering her advice, and it strikes me that most of the audience looks as if it drove in from someplace even more rural, that we're among Appalachia's rock fans, people traveling to this site the way ranch hands ride into town on Saturday in western movies.

Eventually Derek spots Aaron and the rest of the band near the stage as they pile out of the old Mazda van we've loaned them. "These hicks," Derek says, "are in for a surprise." By this time, nearly seven o'clock, the idea of Strangers With Candy playing here seems suddenly fortunate. More than a hundred additional cars and pickup trucks have pulled in and parked on the hillside above us. The edgy, raw music Strangers With Candy will be playing in just over an hour has the kind of insistent rhythm, I imagine, that will pull all of these people to their feet and toward the stage, get them to say, "Who are these guys?" even before Nick commands them, "I want to see all you motherfuckers go crazy out there."

By now I'm so bored with hearing covers of the music Derek played in his room during middle school that I'm relieved when the singer announces, "This is our last tune." They sputter into "Dirty White Boys," an old song by Foreigner. "Hell, yeah," roars a small group of bottle-carrying men nearby. "I need a clean, white bitch," one says, and three women sitting together on a blanket giggle as if they're playing in a sandbox. I watch Aaron and the rest of the band open the old blue van, getting ready to unload their equipment. In a minute, I think, I'll shake hands with all of them on my way to refill the pathetic eight-ounce plastic cup I drained two minutes after I'd waited through three songs to have it filled at a tap regulated by a woman dressed for a Dale Evans look-alike contest.

Halfway through the song the drummer slumps sideways and tumbles to the stage. The guitarists and the vocalist turn, muddling to a stop. "What happened?" my wife says, and I take a couple of steps forward as if shaving five feet from the distance will clarify everything. In less than a minute two attendants materialize and begin to administer CPR.

From where I'm standing, I can tell things aren't going well. Five minutes go by. Ten. The nearest ambulance will take a long time getting this far out into the country. Quiet for most of those ten minutes, the crowd begins to talk and move. "He had heart trouble," I hear one of the women on the blanket say. "And he was smoking up there the whole time."

"His wife's up there with him," the woman beside her says. But though they speak of the drummer as if he lives in their neighborhood, none of them have stood up to get a better look.

"Fucking stone, man," one of the bottle-holding guys announces. A second one nods. "Fucking ton of bricks."

Derek glances at them and says to me, "I can't listen to this bullshit." He walks toward where Aaron and the band are standing. Hundreds of people surge to form lines at the beer taps; I start paying attention to the audience.

The nearby analysts pivot and start hollering in unison, and I turn to see a huge, bearded man in a Lynrd Skynrd T-shirt waving a liquor bottle like a baton. I listen, pick up enough of his bellowing to decipher a drinking cheer complete with screams for vodka and tequila. The would-be clean, white bitches on the blanket take a break from their dialogue about the health and family of the drummer to giggle again.

"What's wrong with these people?" my wife says. I watch a couple of younger guys begin to toss a miniature football. They jog through simple patterns, darting, then hooking among blanket sitters. As soon as the ball is dropped, tumbling loose along the ground, the game expands, the ball heaved through the crowd to hands held high overhead. I notice couples on several blankets close in on each other, count a dozen staggering drunks, and listen to hundreds of audible obscenities, *fuck* being chief among them.

In fact, at Wilapalooza *fuck* seems more frequent and various in its uses than the verb "to be." Besides being tossed as a verb as easily as that football, it's an adjective and an adverb: "That fucking band must be bummed out" and "This fucking sucks." Ultimately, though, it's all-purpose, spanning the sludge of inept grammar like a makeshift bridge: "Get the fuck out of here." "No fucking way." "Fuck yeah." "Fucking throw me the fucking ball." Suddenly, these people look like nobody I ever talk to, nobody I would ever see unless I stood on this hillside. Except for the occasional hulk, the men are uniformly skinny, mustached with hair long in the back and short on the sides, hanging on to the mullet hair style favored by country singers who competed with Tom Petty in 1982 if they wanted a crossover hit. The women, on the other hand, come in two sizes—emaciated and obese—and they're so pale they look as if they've dragged themselves away from months of steady television for this one summer day outside.

Don't be such a judge, I tell myself, but perhaps a hundred people aside, the crowd has turned indifferent, impatient, and obnoxious. "What you lookin' at?" repeats itself through the lips of two men within earshot. I imagine it spreading across the hillside like a rash, somebody inevitably scratching at it hard enough to draw blood, but despite all those internal cautions, I find myself staring at one of them, a man in his twenties who has his hand under a woman's shirt.

Eyeing me suddenly, the man spits out, "What you doing here, you old fuck? You trying to get laid?" He doesn't take his hand out from under the woman's shirt, and she turns slowly, looking me up and down before she grunts a disapproval.

"My son's in one of the bands."

"He shouldn't quit his day job then."

"You haven't heard them yet."

"What the fuck band is it?"

"Forget it."

"Exactly. You lame fuck," he says, thankfully turning back to the pleasures of fondling.

Derek, Aaron, and the rest of Strangers With Candy trek up the hillside. The ambulance, after twenty minutes, has come and gone, CPR continuing in a way that makes me think *hopeless.*

"They want us to go on next because the band that's scheduled knows the guy who just went down," Aaron says to me. "I don't want to play. What do you think?"

I think about the thousand or more people who will hear him in an hour. I consider the publicity their performance will generate in a part of the state where they haven't played before. I'm uncomfortable saying it, but I tell him he should play.

"Nobody should be listening to music like ours tonight," Aaron says, the rest of the band and Derek nodding. I conjure the Oompa Loompas, the calls to "break stuff" and "jump around," and I back off enough to say, "It's up to you," bringing on a few seconds of ground scuffling.

Mark looks pale. He suddenly sits down and begins to stare at the ground. I see all the signs of an anxiety attack, the kind of embarrassment I'm prone to. Hyperventilating. Going cold and clammy, blood pressure dropping as if your circulatory system has sprung a leak.

"Breathe in a bag if you can find one," I offer like a talk-radio health-show host. "That's what I learned in the emergency room one night."

He glances up and nods, but I can tell my stupid cure-all isn't sinking in. "This is completely fucked up," Nick says. He's wearing a simple red T-shirt; all of them look like they're here for fried chicken, baked beans, and lemonade. And when Mark doesn't resist, Chris and Aaron lift him to his feet, and the band heads back toward the stage.

"Aaron's right, Dad," Derek says. "They should say 'screw it' and get out of here."

I crush my plastic cup and let it fall to the ground, adding one more item to the spreading litter. Two more bottle-carriers stumble in front of us as if we've called them with a dog whistle for drunks. The taller one, thin as an AIDS victim, taps his bottle against the chest of the other. "Captain Morgan on board," he says.

The second man salutes, remembering, at least, to raise his empty hand to his forehead. "Jack Daniels ready for orders, sir," he says.

They look over at three men sitting in chairs. "You fucking pussy drinkers," Captain Morgan says. "Beer in a cup." He tilts the bottle and swallows. "Faggots," he finishes. "This ain't no church picnic."

The three men stare at the stage. One of them holds a Black Lab on a chain leash, and I imagine him whispering "Tear their throats out" into its ear and releasing the catch on its collar.

The drummer's death (anyone could tell), according to crowd behavior, has been almost unanimously forgotten. The long break has accelerated the drinking. By now I spot three different sets of men wrestling, against a background of innuendo-laced comments to women. The women almost always yell back. Firecrackers and sparklers are tossed. Unaffected whatsoever by the incident, a few spectators sprawl in stupors they entered while the drummer was still keeping time.

In the five minutes it takes for Aaron and the rest of the band to zigzag their way through the impatient crowd, I have enough time to prepare excuses, rationalizations, and justifications for waffling on their reluctance to perform. I tell myself to find men in this crowd who remain subdued. Surely they are present. My wife tugs my arm. "Stop it," she says, and I nod, understanding even without an antecedent. "We'll see them again," she adds.

"Maybe."

I watch a woman in a halter top rest her hand high on the thigh of a man in jeans. The man rolls over and pulls a blanket up around them. A minute later the blanket pops open and the woman wipes her mouth with the back of her hand while the man brings a bottle of vodka to his lips and drinks. Sitting up, then standing, the woman looks unsteady, and her bare stomach oozes over the waistband of her skin-tight purple slacks "Fuck," the woman says. "This is boring."

And, fortunately, the five minutes I've spent following their sexual adventure is also long enough for me to recognize the selfishness of every expedient reason I've formed for suggesting that Strangers With Candy perform. In fact, I eventually form the word *asshole* to describe myself, because if I had heard a father encouraging his son to play fifty minutes of rap-metal music to this crowd of hard-core drunks, I would have labeled him less kindly than that.

From the stage area, my son catches our attention, turning a thumbs down. "Good call," Derek says, and I nod, then watch the van pull out and leave. In another five minutes, when I see the promoter has talked another band into setting up, I'm ready to follow.

For a few minutes, not moving, I watch their hurried preparations until Derek reminds me I'm lapsing into voyeur mode. "Okay," I say, turning. As we gather our two blankets the band on stage begins to labor through their original material. They sound dreadful, but the crowd, as darkness settles in and we work our way up the littered hillside, roars at the end of both songs we hear as if Led Zepplin has reunited and added Wila, Pennsylvania, to their cross-country summer tour.

Back at the car I see three hard-asses sitting on the tailgate of a nearby Ford pickup. Each of them is holding a bottle of Bacardi 151. "This fucking band fucking sucks fucking ass," one says. I make sure to avoid eye contact, and I estimate another hundred people are sweeping in over the hillside to my left. It's nearly dark. The band, perhaps reading the minds of a thousand all-day drinkers, switches to covers, beginning with "Brown Sugar," a change that brings a mock cheer from the bust-head rum guzzlers.

One of them reaches down and picks up an empty bottle from the truck bed. He flings it in an arc so high it carries only one row of cars toward the stage, splintering into hundreds of shards when it lands on the extended cab of a muddy Chevy pickup.

"Like a rock," one of the others yells. All three of them whoop, and I wager with myself that the band on stage will cover Bob Seger before their set ends. And then I'm in my car, my wife already smoothing out the map under the dome light, Derek slipping on headphones to choose his own concert. A minute later I turn left onto Elk Road like I clearly remember. I pay attention to every upcoming road sign because I need to get every turn correct in order to prove something important to myself.

These Guys Rule

"You guyz bring some real talent to the area." — gr8ful, a fan

In September, after the band had stayed "huge" for a month, Aaron, as he had promised to do, gives notice at Gelnett. "I think I can make a living at this," he says. "I'm going to move to Wilkes-Barre and see what happens. Chris is leaving, too."

I ask him how the news went over with the other workers at Gelnett, and Aaron frowns. "Most of those guys gave me that look, you know the one. 'You'll be back,' they said."

A few weeks later, when we sit in a pizza shop six blocks from where his apartment is in Wilkes-Barre, Aaron shows me the Media Five ad for Strangers With Candy. There they are, the four of them with their hands outstretched from behind prison bars. "We did a shoot inside the old jail," he says. "Fourteen," he says, counting the October dates, and I do some quick, crude math when he tells me his rent and what they're paid, on average, by those clubs. I double the rent money, throw in a hundred dollars for the kind of expenses a twenty-two-year-old thinks are necessary, and make that my guess of what it takes to get by.

"You need about ten dates a month to pay room and board," I say.

He doesn't argue. Instead he shows me the ads for other local bands. "Six dates," he says. "These guys better have second jobs. Look at these bands—eight dates, nine, eleven. There's only one band listed here with more dates than us. This won't slow down."

Before they finish those October dates, they get a new member, Tony (aka DJ Worm), who joins them in Allentown at a club called Crocodile Rock. So they have turntables now, and for sure, Tony is excited. When Nick orders drinks from the bar between sets, Aaron tells me the next day, Tony joins in and they run a tab that, by the end of the night, totals $200.

"Nick started bitching," Aaron says. "You can imagine. 'We're the band,' he said, as if that explained everything, but it was no-go with the manager. It was all downhill after that."

I listen as Aaron describes how the club was decorated for Halloween, pumpkins and cornstalks and all the rest surrounding the outside of the building. "Nick and Tony hefted a few of those pumpkins, and you just knew this was going to get stupid," Aaron says. "Pretty soon they started heaving them at the club. Nothing got broken except all those pumpkins, but the club was a major mess."

"And then you made your escape?" I say.

"So we thought. But today came the phone call from Media Five. 'You know anything about smashed pumpkins?' they asked Nick. 'No,' Nick said, but it was a bad time to lie. The club has security cameras. Nick and Tony are on film. They looked like amateur bank robbers, Media Five said. They looked like idiots. There goes another club off the booking list."

"What's up with DJ Worm now?"

"He stays."

I shake my head. "Why does a rock band need a DJ?"

"Trust me," Aaron says. "Except for adding another split to the money, it helps."

Within a few weeks, they manage another milestone—opening for a signed band. "Bif Naked," Aaron says, and though I've been paying close attention to alternative rock, nothing registers.

"She's all over MTV," Aaron adds, sensing my ignorance. "This is huge for us. We're playing at some big resort, skiing or something."

I see photographs before Aaron calls again. Two days after the show a fan site posts Bif Naked and Strangers With Candy pictures. Everybody in the band looks happy, the way, five years before, Aaron and the rest of his high school band Seed looked the night they played with the Badlees, the Central Pennsylvania band that was about to go national as part of the roots-rock phenomenon. The biggest difference is that everybody is holding a drink and sporting at least two choices from the three-item rock and roll menu of tattoos; spiked, dyed hair; and multiple piercings.

Aaron calls that night. "Bif Naked was cool. She gave us respect."

"Good," I say.

"It was a little lame, though," Aaron says. "Nobody came. It was at that ski resort, you know, and there was maybe fifty people. We're used to it, so it was cool for us, but she must have wondered what was up."

"So MTV isn't a magic wand?"

"You'd think," Aaron says. "But there it was. Maybe if it was snowing or something, people would have gotten into it at a place like that."

The off-season. In late November, Strangers With Candy plays to three people in Wildwood, New Jersey. "The smallest crowd of all time," Aaron reports. "Who goes to the shore when it's freezing outside?"

"It sounds like a poetry-reading crowd," I say, but Aaron lets my literary joke thud to the ground.

"This place was clueless, Dad," he says. "There was a huge banner across the wall behind us. You know what it said? 'Strangers With Candy—Alternative Dance Band.'" He pauses for a moment. "Yeah," he adds finally. "What's that?"

"There's always a really drunk chick." – everybody in the band

On Thanksgiving night, in Wilkes-Barre, she's the first person to dance in front of the stage, dragging a guy with her when Strangers With Candy launches into their third song, a White Zombie cover. And whether it's her gyrations and suggestive hip thrusts or the crowd loosening up, the song ends to scattered applause and whoops of appreciation instead of the silence that ended the first two covers.

During the next song, the first time I've ever heard "Boring," the band's new original, the girl stops in front of Nick, her arms raised so her breasts lift and press against her T-shirt, and she stands there for a minute in that pose while the guy she's with pretends he's still dancing with somebody. It's not quite 11 P.M., and she's in a zone that squeezes attention out of even the heaviest drinkers, some of whom are creeping closer to the stage, gradually filling the room as uniformly as a diffusion experiment.

She collapses back into something animate, and then she takes the plastic cup of beer from the guy's hand, walks to the front of the stage, and pours the beer over her head, leaning back so it sops into her shirt. "What's going on with you, girl?" Nick asks, and she shrieks "Tonya" in a voice designed by alcohol.

The crowd closes in some more, but there's room enough to see she's pulled her shirt up under her breasts and is trying to tie it off like a homemade halter top. The guy she's with is bouncing off the half dozen others in the first small mosh pit of the night, but she's hearing something slow and provocative in the Korn cover the band is playing, and she does a series of backbends, arching far enough to lift that shirt over her breasts, holding her position so long a bouncer steps forward, nudges her upright and begins to talk directly into her ear.

So it's no surprise that when Tammy, the first contestant in the between-sets wet T-shirt contest is finished being splashed by water as she grinds to some hip-hop beat, Tonya steps up as contestant number two. Her back arch is unmistakable. She looks like fountain architecture, something that will spew water upward from her mouth after it floods over her body from a half dozen large cups. Nick, wearing a shirt that inexplicably says I'M NOT EUGENE, rushes to pour a cup over her, carefully dividing the water between both breasts. Five minutes later, Tonya wins by acclamation, though nobody lets us know what her prize is besides being briefly in a hundred sex fantasies.

Two songs into the second set Tonya bounces onto the stage, her shirt still dramatically soaked. She leans into Nick, whispers into his ear, and he says "Connie" into the mike. Tonya is triumphant. "He wants Connie," she squeals into the mike and then stays on stage, throwing herself into a caricature of go-go dancing during "Bulls on Parade."

Aaron cranks the opening riff of "Break Stuff," and this time she slides his way during the song, leaning so far to the side she seems to be pressing her body against him for balance. I move forward to evaluate her expression, and it looks exactly like the face of someone whose next coherent thought will arrive after ten hours of sleep.

When Aaron keeps a straight face, finishing "Break Stuff" as if she's a computer-generated hologram, she throws herself on Nick again between songs, rubbing against him, squealing into the mike "Look at how cute he is," which finally raises a chorus of "Get the fuck off the stage."

Which she does, one song later, lifted by a bouncer, walked through the air, and dropped behind the crowd to my right. I don't see Tonya again until the crowd parts five minutes later because she's dropped to her knees to throw up.

Thanksgiving dinner, I think. Turkey and gravy, mashed potatoes and pumpkin pie.

"The fastest rising musical force in Northeast Pennsylvania"
— ad copy. Strangers With Candy

Derek designs a logo for the band, stark and stylized lowercase lettering that looks striking on the black T-shirts they begin to sell. On the back is a cartoonish predator following two young children, a tableau just this side of bad taste.

He works for an advertising agency, takes on responsibility for their ad copy as well: "Strangers With Candy slides effortlessly between genres, mixing up high-energy shows with flawlessly faithful covers, new takes on band favorites, and hard-hitting originals." On this flyer they stand outside the prison rather than reach out from inside a cell. I have two of the T-shirts, and I wear them like billboards.

But not everything is going well. "Listen to this," Aaron says. "We play at this club every week, and last week when we're loading out, Chris is missing a stack of CDs."

"Why does he take CDs to a show?"

"You know, we play them before the show and in-between sets. They were just gone at the end of the night. Of course, nobody at the club knows anything."

"Anybody could have taken them," I offer.

"Yeah, except last night we played there and those CDs are in the jukebox now."

"That's not good," I say, buying time to consider advice.

"We're missing T-shirts, too. The guy's out of line."

"That's what a manager's for—doesn't Media Five book more than you guys into that club? Can't they threaten to spread the word and screw him?"

"This is way beyond a manager doing a job, Dad."

I look at my son, and I feel like a father who believes drinking beer is a problem until he finds out those were the good nights.

"Listen, Dad, he rips us off on head count. We get a flat rate and then a bonus based on the size of the crowd."

"That's a good thing for you guys now, isn't it? You're packing them in."

"Yeah," Aaron says. "Sort of. It's like being a waiter. You accept shitty pay with the idea you can make big tips, but one of the bouncers told us he's ordered to not count every fifth person who comes in. So if there are five hundred fans, we get a dollar a head for four hundred. A hundred dollars—we're making him a shitload of money packing the house and boosting the bar tab, and he's saving a hundred dollars."

"What can you do?"

"That's right. What can we do. This guy keeps a gun on the table when he pays us. I'm not bullshitting you. He thinks he's Tony Soprano. Everything's in cash, no questions expected. You think Media Five is going to bring up a hundred dollars?"

And when Aaron visits for Christmas, he owns up to worrying about money. Three months living on his own, and he realizes that one month of short playing dates, December dropping to eight bookings, is enough to run his savings down to week-to-week. "It's not a crisis yet," he says, "but January's looking thin, too, seven or eight shows, so I'm worried maybe this won't last after all. And now we have all these originals we play and no money for studio time just when we have something going on."

"I have money," I say at once, quickly adding, "up to a point."

Aaron perks up. "You'd front money for a CD?"

"I've seen enough," I say. "I've heard those originals. If nothing else, you should record in case the whole thing blows up." And then, taking a breath, I say, "What's something like that cost?"

"$1,900 to record seven songs. $3,000 to produce 2,000 CDs."

"You've been doing the homework," I say. "I'm good with those numbers. What's that make me—the executive producer? You'll sell enough CDs to pay me back, and then you guys can keep the profits. Go ahead and book time."

Ultimate Cover Band

When the phone jars me awake at 2:13 A.M., I'm out of bed and in the kitchen before the third ring leaps through the dark. "They won," my daughter says, and I carry the phone to a comfortable chair, ready to listen for as long as it takes her to detail how she and her husband eyewitnessed her brother's extraordinary night.

"TALENT," she says, her voice in capital letters in the early morning darkness. "That's what was printed on our passes. They looked the same as Aaron's." I nod as if she could hear it. Aaron gets to wear one because he plays guitar in Strangers With Candy; the other band members sport the tags as well. But, happily, Shannon and her husband, David, possess them, too, since the band received five extra passes, and three of the band members know nobody in New York to give them to.

I hear David pick up on their other line as I think of how a single word can be nearly as powerful as "open sesame" if it's printed on a laminated tag and dangles in plain sight of security guards. "Our pass opened every door but one in the Roseland Ballroom," she says, beginning to elaborate on the two days it took to rehearse and tape the MTV's Ultimate Cover Band Battle.

"You don't have to tell me about the part I'll see," I say. "Let that be a surprise."

"All tens," she says. "They got all tens every time from every judge."

"Great," I say, "but tell me the other stuff."

"Okay. Here's something. It's one time the bouncers were nice. They smiled and talked."

"Even better," David says, interrupting, "the first day they automatically thought I was with the band."

So the two of them have had access to all the preparation as well as a view of the show from a restricted area above and just to the side of the celebrity judges. David has even snapped pictures of the filming on rehearsal and interview day. Which is at least part of what I suddenly want to know, because I want to learn what will be edited out of the television show. I want to understand how people act off camera, what happens in real time while Strangers With Candy plays covers of rock, hip-hop, and pop songs for millions of MTV viewers.

David tells me the MTV stylist had the band lay out everything they'd brought from Wilkes-Barre to New York. Not much, it turned out: T-shirts, a change of pants. The band members had packed, if they'd packed at all, as if they were staying overnight for a two-day picnic.

Aaron's Superman shirt survived the cut, David says. So did Nick's black vinyl jacket. Mark and Tony's small wardrobe of caps. The stylist took Polaroids of the band, studied Mark and Chris, asked a few questions about what the band liked to wear, and went off to buy clothes at Urban Outfitters.

Despite the time, David seems ready to give an hour-by-hour report. Most of the first day, he says, was a long walk-through of the show. Where to stand. Where Tony should set up his turntables. Where to move and how quickly, especially when your band is eliminated.

Shannon and David both insist they didn't mind the standing around. Displaying their TALENT tags, they returned as soon as they could the following day, which, given the hour, is now yesterday. Even better, for everybody wearing a TALENT pass, dinner was courtesy of MTV. The food arrived by truck, Shannon says, and though the choices were varied and well prepared, it was "served" on the street outside at six o'clock during the first week of a New York City February. "Cold as hell," Shannon summarizes, "but I got chicken and mashed potatoes and gravy, so I was good with it."

After dinner, David says, the stylist took over. He starts to quote her as if she spoke in memorable phrases: "'If you're wearing orange over here,'" she said to Aaron, "'the other orange is over there,'" and pointed toward Mark and Tony. She banned polka dots, stripes, and the color red: "'It doesn't work for television.'" She made it clear that she understood the nature of color and size coming through a television screen, and the band, eventually, gave itself up to her. Even Aaron surrendered and wore Tony's pants because Tony wears them baggier and he's thicker than Aaron, so they'll look even more baggy—read trendy—on Aaron."

David pauses, and for a moment I think he realizes he's run on for a minute about detail so trivial I might be checking the clock and reconsidering the time of night. "Half an hour until they play is no time to argue or pout or lose concentration," he says quickly. "She tucked the tags in before they went on stage."

"'I have to return this stuff tomorrow,'" Shannon quotes her. "'And when the band looked surprised, she had to explain herself: 'I can't go to the same store too many times. If the salespeople recognize me, they won't serve me.'"

Because I want to know everything, and it's going on 3 A.M., Shannon says she'll draw me a sketch of the Roseland Ballroom and mail it to me with an explanation of where they stood before, during, and after. She's an artist, and I imagine the things that matter in the interior taking shape rapidly. Her pen will do more to make things clear than her rapid-fire talk: "A camera on a crane swung from side to side. Then it swooped up and down. You know. It moved all around."

"We were almost right above the judges," she finally says, coming back to something I can picture. "If you wanted to assassinate Ahmet Zappa, all you needed was a TALENT pass. Nobody questioned us."

When I ask what might seem least realistic on television, Shannon says, "The crowd near the end when Strangers plays 'Nookie.' A lot of people left before it was over. It's Wednesday night. At least it was until a couple of hours ago. There were kids who had school the next day, people who had to work. And then there was a forty-five-minute delay after The Zoo—you'll see who they are—got a perfect score in the last round, because MTV didn't have a way to deal with a possible tie. If you can believe it, they had the crowd cheer to choose a winner, and you better believe that was risky because Roseland was way fuller an hour earlier."

"Definitely, we were worried at the end," David says. "The Zoo was from Long Island and had a bunch of fans there. Strangers had like maybe ten people altogether."

"Okay," I say, and they both seem to sense they've given away the ending.

"We should stop," Shannon says. "It's like 3 A.M. or something, and pretty soon you won't need to watch the show."

"**When I look** at the television, I want to see me staring right back at me," sings Adam Duritz of Counting Crows, and sure enough, ten days after I get that first report, I know my son Aaron and the rest of Strangers With Candy are in Wilkes-Barre watching themselves perform on MTV at the same time I'm settling in to watch in my basement. I'm so trained in allusions it's the first thing I think when the band is about to perform. Since I know beforehand they're going to win, I'm relaxed, making an enormous tray of nacho supreme with Derek. We pile on cheese and hamburger and tomatoes and hot peppers, everything we love. I drink beer like a teenager, fast and talking all the while, making sure all of this comes ready at 1:55 when we go downstairs, get the volume pumping through the stereo speakers, set the VCR to record and, at 1:59, turn it on manually, sit back, and say "Yesss!" together as if Beavis and Butthead themselves have taken over our psyches.

By now, because Shannon and David have called back twice since the night of the taping, I not only know the results, I know exactly what the band performed. And because Aaron has called, talking a nonstop half hour for once, I even know what songs the other four bands played, what the hosts said, how the bands were judged and what was said to them. But as soon as the first band (The Zoo) is introduced, I'm suddenly nervous, as if somehow the show could be changed. It strikes me as odd and disorienting to settle down in front of a medium that produces widespread fame and recognize my son. Because I know him and the other band members, it's as if I'm looking down a tunnel to New York City, seeing them live rather than watching film that has been edited and shaped to fit the format of a two-hour show. And no matter what anybody has told me, I have to see the show to its very end before I believe in the outcome. My wife, my friend Tom, Derek, and Keri watch as well, but I'm transfixed, gobbling nachos, swilling beer, and turning up the volume another seven notches when Strangers With Candy, the last band to perform in each round, is finally about to play "Guerilla Radio."

"Our next band is from Pennsylvania," Ahmet Zappa, the MTV host says, "and they are Strangers With Candy. Rock . . . out."

And when Nick pivots and leaps and lets loose with four guttural roars, the TALENT ID tag hanging from his neck flapping in front of his face, the wifebeater he's wearing nearly glowing when his orange sweatshirt flies apart, they do. "Lights out / Guerilla radio / Turn that shit up," Nick screams, the obscenity barely blipped out, and a mosh pit forms in the surging crowd.

In exactly forty-five seconds Strangers With Candy's performance ends. Striding among the band, Ahmet Zappa shouts, "Strangers With Candy . . . raw! You guys rock!" Aaron lifts his guitar over his head and waits, like the other four band members, for the three celebrity judges to rate them.

Eve, a rap artist, blurts, "I was feelin' y'all. I was feelin' y'all," and holds up a card that reads *10*.

Mandy Moore, a teen pop singer, beams and babbles, "You guys totally rocked. Your outfits are kickin.' Ten all the way."

Strangers With Candy is two-thirds of the way to the perfect score that's confirmed, after he gives a pompous-sounding harangue about how music isn't a competition, by Stephan Jenkins of Third Eye Blind.

Even then, I hold my breath, watching in an entirely different way than my daughter and her husband have watched. They saw nearly everything. I see what MTV chooses for me to see. "Who is that guy that talks too much?" Tom asks during the commercials that follow the first round, the all-girl band eliminated. "What's he mean about music not being a competition? Where does he think he is?"

Liz walks upstairs to gather us a fresh round of beers. "A special time," she says, as if that explains her willingness.

"Stephan Jenkins looks drunk," Derek says.

"Is that his name?" Tom says, and I smile, thinking of how Stephan Jenkins would feel about being as anonymous as a worker bee to someone watching this show.

"Welllllll . . . Bam!" Eve shouts, holding up another ten for Strangers With Candy when they finish covering House of Pain's "Jump Around." "What I'm sayin' is I like y'all." Mandy Moore holds up a ten. Stephan Jenkins, undeterred, gives another speech about the joys of making your own music before he raises his ten to the camera.

"Genius. Genius," Ahmet Zappa gushes as the band finishes its "pop cover." "Oh yes, Strangers With Candy giving us a genius version of 'Take On Me.'"

A moment later, in the middle of another set of tens, Mandy Moore says, "You guys have talent. I don't know . . . everywhere," but even this deep into the show, it's only when the commercials are on that I relax, running upstairs for the next round of beer. I've leaned forward every time one of those judges has lifted a card, exhaling at each perfect score as if MTV might have retouched them to read something other than *10*.

And finally I'm grateful that Shannon and David and Aaron have all told me that both The Zoo and Strangers With Candy get all tens for their last cover. Without knowing the outcome, I would have fallen into despair when The Zoo, before Strangers With Candy, plays and totals thirty, an insurmountable score, for covering a medley of Lit and Harvey Danger. Now I can concentrate on the band, give myself up to the cover of "Nookie," and wait for the tens to be held up as uniformly as the votes from the Communist Bloc Olympics judges of my childhood.

And when the phone rings, as the credits roll, it's my son the guitarist talking from Wilkes-Barre, where he really lives, asking me what I think as his image continues to smile from the screen. I know a television is on where he's calling from, that he's staring at himself as we speak.

The beeps of call waiting sound through the phone, and I guess it is my daughter calling from New York, completing the cycle, the technology of pride and love, some enormous loop of time and space, holding the afternoon together.

At school, on Monday, I get a second copy of the videotape made in the university's media center. During class I imagine my recording being somehow snagged in the Media Center's equipment and unwinding into a snarl of uselessness. I run errands to prepare for the first day of tennis, the practice that will begin my twentieth season of coaching, but by three o'clock, unable to do anything but be a father, I retrieve the new copy and slide it into the VCR in the English Department's seminar room and invite my colleagues to see the band perform.

The secretary obliges me, coming as far as the doorway. "Oh my, Gary," she says, her hands braced against the doorframe, and when the phone rings in her office, she seems relieved. One colleague pokes his head in the door. "Is that your son?" he says, and when I nod, he smiles benignly and shuffles off to reread Jane Austen. No one else even pretends to watch.

I let the volume slide up a few more notches just as the one English major among my tennis players walks by. "Coach," he says, "I heard about your son's band on MTV. Is this it?"

"Yeah."

"And they won?"

"Yeah."

"That's so freaking great," he says, shutting the door. "Turn it up."

Derek designs the cover art for the CD Strangers With Candy begins to record the week after the MTV show. "I want whoever looks at the cover to think sex," he says, and he spends night after night at his coworker's house, the two of them drinking beer and designing possibilities until Derek decides on a flower that appears to be just unfurled.

"Young and female," I think, recalling a myriad of sex-suggestive flowers painted by Georgia O'Keefe. "It works," I say aloud.

He shows me the inside art, a hand creeping under the waistband of panties. "It works even better," I say, and let it go.

I look at the liner copy, a jumble of acknowledgements that sounds like an Oscar acceptance speech gone on too long. Where the band members' names are listed, I see Nic, Chris, Mark, Worm, and Rinn.

"Rinn?" I say. "Since when?"

"They want just first names. And nothing about what they do in the band. They need to see the light on this."

"When is it due?"

"Tomorrow. I already have revised copy for when they come to their senses."

I think of them refusing to change, approving copy that lists them as if the band were made up of household pets. I'm relieved, a day later, when Derek convinces them that someone other than the fans who travel to every show within a hundred miles might buy this CD called *No Need*.

And somebody else does. The CD opens at #4 in northeast Pennsylvania, falling just behind the one by Sisqó that features "The Thong Song." And when they play a high school show, selling out the auditorium for charity, putting on a PG-rated performance, Nick singing and talking for two hours without ever once blurting the word "fuck," a hundred of those teenagers rush to buy a copy of *No Need*.

The next day, when Aaron says they'll be sold out of CDs in a couple of weeks, I tell him to make two thousand more, and I write him another check. "And get more T-shirts made," I say. "Send me the bill."

For once I feel like a fortune teller when I predict I'll get all this additional money back in three months. Even better, within six weeks I'm in the clear. Strangers With Candy sells $11,000 worth of merchandise, pays me, and begins to make a profit.

Fan sites spring up on the Internet. "I was like oh my god these guys totally kick fucking ass. Who are they?" says Kyra. "This band is in-fucking-credible," Lysa submits.

Each time I check, one new message after another scrolls down the screen: "Dudes—you are destined for greatness!" "You guys kill." "If any of you want to come to my prom with me, let me know."

I read them every day, including the ones that fantasize how good my son would be in bed, but a month after the MTV show has aired and been repeated half a dozen times I know only three people within fifteen years of my age who might have watched it from beginning to end: Tom, the other writer in the department, who watched with us in February; the colleague in the office across the hall who said, the following Monday, "Excuse me for saying this, but it seemed like it was rigged"; and my sister, who told me my father saw "part of it" before he drove home. "I tried to tape it," she said, "but I'm not sure it came out."

She says this both the day after and the week after the show first airs, so I know she hasn't taped it, that most likely she didn't watch the whole way through, that the show was simply on while she busied herself with other things like cleaning the stove or walking the dog. And certainly my father, weeks later, hasn't requested a reshowing.

So when I announce I'm coming to Pittsburgh, an advance pressing of the all-originals Strangers With Candy CD I've fronted the money for in hand, I add, "Should I bring a copy of the MTV thing?"

It's been four weeks by now, and she answers, "It turns out it didn't record."

"Fine," I say, maturely keeping expletives to myself.

Only my father is at my sister's house when I arrive. When I ask him where she keeps her remote, he looks as if I'd asked him for directions to the remains of Noah's Ark. I take this to mean that my sister, like my father, doesn't own one.

It turns out to be a hell of a job setting up the tape. The VCR isn't situated for frequent use. It's three inches off the floor, under the television, under magazines, under anything that needs stacked out of the way. I have to lie down on the carpet to make out the tiny letter-ing for *fast forward* and *play,* and I'm still fiddling and squinting when my sister's husband comes home from work.

He stares at me as if I were lifting his VCR into a duffel bag already sagging under the weight of silverware and jewelry. "I'm get-ting this ready to give Dad a second look at Aaron on MTV."

He grimaces as I push play and a band called Hyperactive appears. "Fine with me," he says, "as long as you keep it on mute."

I lean on one elbow, watching Hyperactive cover a song by No Doubt. The volume, when I press the button, shows eight bars across the screen. "Here's the remote," he says, lifting it from under the chair where it's tucked away, apparently to keep anyone but field mice from seeing it.

My father stares, leaning on the back of a chair to keep his weight off his ruined knees. "Where's Aaron?" he asks, as Hyperactive finish-es, and I know this is going to be complicated.

"That was another band," I say, sliding the volume up to 15, then 20, so he can hear at least muffled babble through the one "partial-hearing" ear he still has at eighty-two.

My brother-in-law frowns as I turn the volume to 25. He's never seen this, I can tell, ignoring it every time it's been repeated on MTV during the past month, yet now he walks into the kitchen to busy him-self making a drink. When Ahmet Zappa appears, Tony just behind him on the screen, I say "Ready?" and rip the volume bars up to 35, then 40, so my father has a slim chance of sensing what "Guerilla Radio" sounds like.

In less than a minute, Strangers With Candy finished, I run the volume back down to 25 and say, "What do you think?"

"This is the part I already saw," he says. "It goes too fast."

I push fast forward as my sister arrives. "He couldn't find Aaron," she says without a prompt.

My father watches the images scampering by at near warp-speed, and I imagine him, in his world of near silence and never owning a VCR, believing his brain has decelerated, that the rest of the world is comfortable following these human chipmunks.

"Okay," I say, pushing play again as Hyperactive, which always performs just before Strangers With Candy, finishes their cover of an old rap tune "Me, Myself, and I." "Aaron will be wearing a Superman shirt this time. He's always on the left of the singer." My father looks as if he's listening through the Urdu earphones at the United Nations, but I turn it up to 40 again, my brother-in-law staying in the kitchen, my sister satisfied to simply make a face, and Strangers With Candy performs "Jump Around" to a trio of anxious body language among which Randall McMurphy would feel at home.

"Everybody jump," Nick screams, "jump up, jump up, and get down." The band gets another set of perfect scores, but nobody in my sister's house utters a word. There's nothing to do but slog on. My father keeps himself propped up through the band's aggressive cover of "Take On Me," and I allow the show to play through so he might hear Eve declare, pointing at Strangers With Candy, "You all need a record deal. For real." On the screen, Aaron beams, and Tony gives one of those mysterious urban hand signs that must, in this context, mean "right on."

After the band covers "Nookie," receiving, as they do each time I replay the tape, their fourth perfect score and the largest share of audience applause, I allow the rest of the show to run toward conclusion as they're announced as winners. "There he is," my father says at last. "There's Aaron," and for sure, there he is, standing behind Ananda the MTV host as she talks the show to a close. For ten seconds he's right behind her shoulder, smiling, and my father seems pleased to finally pick him out.

My sister spots the band's CD on the counter. "We don't own a CD player," she says. "I don't know how you're going to play that."

"In the car," I say. "There's six speakers in the Celica, and two of them are on the side with Dad's good ear. You want to go for a ride and take advantage of all six?"

"No thanks," she says, "I've heard enough for one day." She turns to wash off lettuce in the sink, leaving me with one last surrogate-mother grimace to file away in the cabinet of annoying images.

"Ready?" I say to my father as I pull out of her driveway after dinner.

My father stares at the road as if he expects a jack-knifing truck to loom out of the darkness. "You do what you want," he says.

I try to estimate the volume that will let him at least sense what the band sounds like, and then, driving him home, I let the CD run its seven-song course, not worrying about his disapproval of questionable language. "Idiot," the last song, repeats "fuck me" dozens of times, but my father is blissful. When it's over, he says, "Somebody likes it, right?"

"They hope so."

"Good. As long as somebody likes it."

"Maybe Judy and John will hear it when the New York Symphony does cover versions for NPR."

My father nods. I could say anything from this direction, tell him Aaron has become drug-addled and contracted AIDS, and he would nod the way he does when I travel to Pittsburgh in the summer to play golf, waiting for the course to appear on the right, for me to park and pay for us to do the one thing we can talk about successfully, since every "good shot" or "tough one" is preceded by a visual clue.

Months later, when I ask Aaron about the MTV experience, he says he doesn't have anything to add. When I prod him, he announces, "It was mostly boring."

"Being on MTV was boring?"

"All we did that first day," Aaron says, "was go through a dress rehearsal. Some interns pretended to be hosts and judges. The bands drew straws to decide who would be eliminated. We came in fourth in the make-believe version, so we only played for two minutes before we just had to watch the rest of it."

I think of Shannon and David, as guests, talking excitedly about every detail of both days, but Aaron, months removed from the show, stays unanimated. "We were happy when we drew fourth place," he goes on. "We didn't want the other bands to hear what we were going to play."

I nod. "It wasn't exciting, Dad. Going into Roseland was exciting. Knowing we were going to play on MTV was exciting. Everything else was just standing around. We performed for ten minutes altogether," he says. "We spent two twelve-hour days getting ready for those ten minutes."

"Do the rest of the guys feel like this?"

"No. Ask them. They loved every minute. They even loved standing there for an hour waiting to be told what to do next."

When I bring up the fact that they were interviewed, Aaron gives in a little. "Okay," he says, "there was fifteen minutes of interviews, too."

He looks at me. "Hey," he says, "MTV was cool. That's just the way everything is. People think going into the studio is great, but it's mostly playing the same thing over and over and then listening to it over and over. It's work. It's MTV, so people think it can't be boring, but it is. Playing the music is what's cool."

"But weren't you nervous?"

"When I saw the other bands' set lists, I thought we would win."

"How do you think that would sound to somebody else?"

"But it's true," Aaron says. "They were playing easy stuff. Harvey Danger. Kid Rock. Every band can play that."

"You think the judges thought that way?"

"I don't know," Aaron says. "I hope so."

"So I had more fun than you did?"

"I've never watched the tape again, if that's what you mean. Except for helping us get signed, I wish we hadn't done the show." When I look incredulous, Aaron elaborates. "Don't get me wrong about this," he says. "It's the whole cover-band thing. If I had thought we were going to be a cover band, I wouldn't have joined in the first place, and there we were—MTV's Ultimate Cover Band."

"You could have lost."

"Then I would have been really pissed."

"You think that sounds arrogant?"

"I want it to sound honest. MTV was great. The people were cool. They kept us fed. But all along it's our music I want to play, and I honest-to-God expected to win."

I nod, but I'm saddened. I recognize that feeling of expectation as my own. How achieving something loses its excitement for me because I expect that achievement before it occurs. Getting a Ph.D., for instance. Publishing a book. By the time those things become likely, my choices are saying "Fine" or turning angry. There are no exclamations of "Incredible!" or "Fuck, yesss!" Those are for major upsets, genuine surprises, flukes. If you're prepared, it's not astonishing to win. It's what you expect to do if you perform. When I tell my wife what Aaron has said, she shakes her head. "You trained him," she says.

I rerun the tape I made of that MTV show. So distant now from that performance, I continue to sit up each time Strangers With Candy begins to play, natural enough perhaps, but I still can't stop paying attention to the judges as if they can somehow alter their scores.

Break Stuff

"My suggestion is to keep your distance, 'cause right now
I'm dangerous." – Limp Bizkit

The bouncers evict fighters. You throw a punch, you're gone.
As far as I can tell, it's a solid policy, because the three guys bounced
from Strangers With Candy's first set are all so belligerent I'm ready
to cheer. One has leaned over a scattering of empty bottles to swing
at a bartender who, apparently, was too slow serving his next beer.
Another has laid into a man flung from the mosh pit.

The third one, seconds after he whips his forearm into the back
of a woman, sending her sprawling to her hands and knees, hurls the
first security guard to reach him away just before a second bouncer
closes in. If he needed evidence that it's a really bad idea to resist a
bouncer, he gets it with a simultaneous pair of hammerlocks, a duet
of "give it the fuck ups," and a shove towards the exit that crunches his
shoulder, his hip, and his knee into the doorframe before he disappears into the early April night.

I'm not surprised. I've gone to ten of these shows since February,
each with a capacity crowd and maximum security. In fact, this night,
as the first of three sets explodes to an end, nobody in the crowd
spends more than a few seconds following the violent conclusion to
the fan's evening. I myself turn back to the music almost as quickly
as the most drunken mosher in the club.

The three guys tossed during the opening set have walked away
easy.

"These jerk offs think a ton of bruises is a badge of honor."
— Phil. a bouncer. Luzerne

61

The bouncers in Luzerne are, the band warned me in the dressing room, the most brutal. "They don't take any shit," Nick explains, and Chris nods. "But what the hell, maybe that's good, because there's no reasoning with some of these drunks."

Aaron follows me out to the open floor in front of the stage and stands beside me just behind the small crowd that has pushed forward for the opening band. The security staff I see are relaxed, probably, I think, because there are fewer than a hundred people paying attention, and only a handful doing anything but modest bouncing in place. "It's Plan 9," Aaron says. "Ben's new band."

Sure enough, Ben, back in Pennsylvania for almost a year now after six months in California, is fronting a new band. He looks half-reincarnated, zombie-pale, and Goth-like, and the band is covering the same music Strangers With Candy does—Rage and Tool, which seems like a bad idea because everyone here will compare their versions to the ones played by Strangers With Candy.

"You know Jeremy, don't you?" Aaron says. "He's the drummer."

I nod, hazily remembering that Jeremy went to high school with Shannon. *Another Selinsgrove rock musician,* I think, but it's an uncomfortable moment to be watching Ben performing covers when I can recall all those originals of his that seemed so promising.

The first fan I notice is lost in himself, slamming into people who simply push him away. There's no camaraderie here, no joy in reciprocal violence. He's a one-man mosh pit, a kind of human mosquito thrashing and squirming and finally hunching himself into a body-block position, thrusting forward and sprawling face-first when he encounters nothing but air.

"It's way too early for somebody to be this drunk and stupid," Aaron leans in to tell me. "Watch."

A bouncer, short but thick through the torso like a beer keg, steps past us as if Aaron directed security. The mosher gets bum-rushed to the door, skidding and giggling.

"That was smooth," I say, but now a woman is losing control, grinding against the stage, then lurching back and screaming, flinging her arms, one of which ends with a longneck bottle. She slaps the bottle into the shoulder of a nearby woman, then spins and raps another woman in the ribs, beer foaming up into a frothy slosh across her shirt. Before Plan 9's cover of a Deftones tune ends, she falls and crawls toward the stage, pulling herself up as if she's ready to bite Ben's ankles. And then she's rousted as well, lifted off her feet by a bouncer with bristly beard stubble that seems cut to the same length as his thinning hair. She doesn't giggle. She kicks and scratches and screams "Fuck you" six times before she's out of earshot.

The rest of the set is uneventful, but as soon as Plan 9 leaves the stage, hundreds of fans surge forward from the back of the club, pushing past and then around us, and Aaron gives me a sheepish grin that says "Good luck" as he weaves toward the dressing room.

I work my way to the wall left of the stage, slide down as far as the third or fourth row of fans so I can watch the hard-core moshers and the way the bouncers work the room. It takes two songs to form an organized pit, and when the third, a cover of Rage Against the Machine's "Freedom," begins, about fifty men and a dozen women start to whirlpool, their crashing and thumping bodies swirling towards the center of the pit. Within a minute, though, the most violent hack through the spontaneous geometry with their fists and elbows, slashing off chunks of furious body-slammers, breaking the pit into irregular pieces.

The bouncers are efficient. They pick out the moshers most likely to injure somebody, the men who look as if they want to inflict genuine pain rather than momentary jolts. But when one guy stumbles into a woman, then spins, when a hand grips his shoulder from behind, to throw a haymaker, two bouncers shoot to either side, pull his arms back into their standard double hammerlock, and drag him, his body banging off rows of knees and hips and finally, far down the wall, into the doorframe.

Because this fan begins to moan loudly, now folded up in the doorway, I follow to see if the bouncers show regret or offer apologies. Ten feet behind them, I stake out a spot in the hallway, happy to be away from the worst of the cigarette smoke, the open door letting it and the music blow right through. I don't hear anything but Strangers With Candy's music as they force the doubled-up fan through the outside door and slam it behind him. Ten minutes later, still loitering in that halfway house for smoke and noise, I have no idea what any of the next three evictees have done, but each one of them gets run down the hall and, accompanied by a chorus of "Get the fuck out," pitched into the parking lot like a trash bag.

An hour and a half later, when I step outside to breathe a bit of fresh air midway through the last set, I'm just far enough from the door to miss being struck by the sprawling body of another one of those drunks. "Now stay the fuck out," the bouncer screams. The guy stays immobile, face down on the asphalt. A change of costume and a ten-gallon hat would transform him into any one of a million extras thrown, over the years, through the swinging doors of a western movie saloon. I think of Dalton, the Patrick Swayze character in *Road House*. As the ultimate head bouncer, his advice was always "Take it outside." The drunks in that movie, however, were dangerous in a cartoonish sort of way, prone to carrying knives. Except for the woman who was tossed early, all these evictees seem used to such treatment, as if the night wasn't a real party unless they were scraped across a surface designed for tire treads and shoe soles.

A ménage á trois stumbles past me, two women swinging from the arms of a man who is ugly enough to play the red herring in a slasher movie. *What's his secret?* I say to myself, but halfway across the parking lot things go suddenly bad. The man pulls away from the women, stumbles back two steps, and then, stepping forward, delivers a full right hook into the nearest woman's jaw, laying her out.

Whoa, I think, but the beer-keg bouncer flies by me, tackles the puncher, and drags him down, rolling him over, applying a hammerlock and a choke hold so efficiently I flinch.

"Motherfucking cocksucking sonofabitch," the other woman, still on her feet, screams, delivering a kick to the man's head with each obscenity. And then, seeing a police car loom out from behind the club, she hollers, "Shit fuck hell piss," accelerating her feet to the beat of the shortened expletives as if she knows she's running out of time to deliver punishment.

There's ambivalence in the small crowd that forms. Sure, the guy was out of line right-hooking her to the ground, but given how things have turned, sides are being taken. I know I'm less certain of who's in the wrong here, bouncer included, since he's slipped in some arm-twisting and head-wrenching and good old-fashioned obscene promises of what will happen to this drunk's private parts if he even thinks of making another bad behavioral decision.

The first police car keeps its headlights on the bouncer and the writhing man while the kicking woman helps her downed friend to her feet. A minute goes by, everything stuck, and then a second police car fills the front entry to the lot, so there's no driving out of here except over an axle-threatening curb.

Seeing where the scene is going, the dozen or so people outside the club lose interest and begin to leave on foot, circling around behind the first squad car to where nearly all of the customer cars are parked. In less than a minute I'm almost alone with the police and their handcuffs and subsequent threats.

The drunk guy topples into the first police car, bloodied, moaning, repeating the word *bitch* as if it were a sort of vengeance itself. The woman who was slugged goes too, hustled to the second car, her friend the kicker alongside, both of them hurling death threats over their shoulders.

From inside I hear the familiar opening riff of "Break Stuff," and I know, from reading the set list earlier, the club will empty four minutes from now. The police are more efficient than the bouncers. A third car arrives, and the other two leave. The cop who slides out to patrol on foot is here to be a presence. He folds his arms and stations himself so close to where I'm standing, I feel like he's about to tell me a story. "Move on now," he says.

"I'm not your problem," I say, trusting the evidence of my sober speech and appearance to convey common sense.

"Now," he says, shortening his directions to language dogs understand.

I manage a smile that locks up halfway to sarcasm. The door swings open, letting out half a dozen fans and Nick's voice growling, "I'm like a chainsaw, I'll skin your ass raw." The policeman turns toward me, and I take the first two steps of acquiescence, leaving him to deal with people, who, it seems to me, want only to find their cars and choose the least dangerous driver to get them home.

"Keeping you busy?" I say, passing the bouncer who tackled the woman-puncher.

He takes two quick steps toward me, his face in sudden close-up. "You fucking with me?" he says.

I hold my ground and manage to say "No."

"Then get it the fuck out of here."

The last fifteen minutes have made Strangers With Candy's music sound different. Now it's like a soundtrack to a B-movie, some direct-to-video potboiler featuring brutal characters and thoughtless violence. If some producer bootlegged a month's worth of shows, he'd have enough music for a lifetime of bottom-shelf sequels.

"These fuckers think they're socially hazardous." – Ron. a bouncer. Allentown

"Huge is too small to describe the bouncers in Allentown," Mark has told me, and that description rears up in the taillights of memory as one of the three enormous bouncers leaning against the stair railing says, "You have a good night."

It's 11:30, early for this club in Allentown, but he thinks I'm leaving because nobody who looks dressed for the golf course would be sticking around for three full sets of rap-metal, moshing, and general chaos.

"I'm just putting these in the car," I say, holding up the complete set of Strangers With Candy shirts—black tee, red tee, and tank top, the last of which hangs like an undershirt for a child. All three of the bouncers grin, which pleases me because each of them is taller than my 6'2", and the smallest one looks to outweigh my 210 by 75 pounds.

On the next block, in the Coastal Mart, I'd be a big man; here, among the three bouncers, I've turned into a stick figure, the undersized beanpole beginning junior high in the same building with seniors who spent hours in the weight room lifting equipment I couldn't budge.

I drop the shirts into the trunk like souvenirs from a national park. "The tank tops are a hit with girls," Mark had said, giving me my samples. "And with us," he'd said, laughing, confident in their tiny size. I've already seen some of these shirts on the bodies of young women inside the club. Not one of them seemed self-conscious, and when I walk back toward the club I follow two women in black halter tops that make the Strangers With Candy tank top look like a nun's habit.

"Things that make you go 'ummm,'" the largest bouncer says to me as they disappear up the stairs.

I cough out a short laugh and feel a sudden ripple of fear as I realize how gigantic this shaved-headed man is. "Don't you take to fighting in there," he says. "The fuckers that fight, they're sorry motherfuckers before too long."

Ten minutes later he stands guard on the stage's apron, five feet from Aaron. During the second song, I follow his gaze and spot a skinny guy who's simply running up behind people and shoving them with both hands. Before the song ends, the shaved-headed guy sweeps that jerk off his feet and out, but when he climbs back on stage a red dot appears on his cheek, then his forehead, and finally, near his eyes. He blinks, and then he shows the agility of a slalom expert as he weaves through a swarm of fans toward the skinny fool who's clutching a laser pen and scrambling back through the door.

The band finishes two originals before the shaved-headed guy strides past me, giving a thumbs up to the three bouncers who stand in front of the stage.

"That fat fuck in the wifebeater we ran? He was just asking for a fucking up." – Jerry, a bouncer, Allentown

Between the second and third sets I slip outside, and when he doesn't object, I stand beside the largest bouncer and ask him how big, exactly, he is. "Six-five," he says, "315." He smiles, and I wonder how many times he's identified himself this way.

Thirty feet away, a man who has followed me out of the club stumbles into the street and then, as if the roadway is more stable than the sidewalk, he steadies himself and walks the middle of one lane into the darkness.

"I went to professional wrestling school," the bouncer says, "but it didn't work out. This shit's easy after that." There's movement in the cemetery across the street, and we make out the man who used the road as a sidewalk.

"How the fuck do I get out of here?" he yells our way.

The bouncer shrugs. "He's not my business when he's fucked up in the graveyard." The door opens and a hand beckons. "Rock and roll," the bouncer says, returning to his post.

I follow, walking back into the dressing room, which is so small I get pressed between Aaron and Nick. "You want another bouncer story?" Nick says. "In New Jersey, last week, two bouncers walked into the lounge at the end of the show, ran me up against the wall, and said they were going to kick my fucking ass."

"Why?"

"They thought I said 'Mess with the bouncers' instead of 'Don't mess with the bouncers' during the last set. What the fuck. It's a good thing the owner walked by and the door was open. Guys like Aaron and Chris couldn't have pried those dudes off me."

Chris, who's stuck sitting on the arm of the couch, nods. "New Jersey," he says. "Remember that place where the bouncer lifted Tony off the ground by his neck?"

"Rude," Nick says.

The good guys, I say to myself, repeating what the band has told me each time I bring up what looks to me like security overkill. "They're the good guys. They keep people off us."

"Like an army," I say aloud. "All that firepower is a comfort if the guns are pointed where you want them to point."

"We're good to go here, though. These guys are righteous."

I manage an unconvinced nod as they make their way back to the stage. *The police aren't scary unless you've done something that makes you afraid of them,* I think, remembering something passed down as an absolute by my father. *Unless they think you've done something,* I say to myself now. *Or worse, unless they think you might do something.* It's an invisible line because it's one you can cross without knowing it—and without moving—just change your expression, just mumble the wrong words, or, in New Jersey, for one night, say the right words and have them heard wrong.

"You don't really know why, but you wanta justify rippin' someone's head off." — Limp Bizkit

In Hazleton, fifteen bouncers (I count them) in red security shirts form a sort of gauntlet as I pass through a lobby and enter an honest-to-God ballroom, glass chandeliers and all. After an aisle of enormous chests and shoulders, it's disorienting to see all that glitter, tables lining all of the walls as if I'd wandered into a senior prom for an alternative school.

It's Easter, but two booths sell beer and mixed drinks, and the lines are long. Above the stage hangs a huge banner reading Coors Light Welcomes Strangers With Candy—NO MOSHING. Above me the largest chandelier dangles as if it is a prop in *The Poseidon Adventure,* something that the extras will fall into when the ship rolls over.

It's a place for dance bands and swing music. Much of the audience looks rural and unsophisticated, people who heard the band won some MTV award and want to check it out. They are sitting at the tables smoking and drinking. I wonder how they'll react when they hear the opening riff of "Keep Away."

A small group wearing Strangers With Candy shirts is already bunching near the stage—the hard-core fans, maybe a hundred of them driving to Hazleton from Wilkes-Barre and Scranton. I recognize Butch and John and Hyland. I see the woman who always wears a tiger-striped halter top and black leather pants, a half dozen women sporting their homemade candy girls T-shirts. When the lights blink off and the band tears into the Godsmack cover, most of the people at the tables stay seated. Those who stand move tentatively into the space behind the regulars, watching them heave against each other as closely as they watch the band.

Despite the first set receiving the quietest reception from an audience I've seen since the MTV show, the bouncers break repeatedly into the knot of playful fans. Within a half hour Butch is carried outside by two bouncers. A moment later he's back, along with the other dozen fans who have been rousted out. As far as I can tell, as soon as a fan makes any sort of physical contact with whoever is bouncing beside them, the security staff grabs him, drags him outside, and threatens him with expulsion.

Overkill, I think, listening. This red-shirted staff gives first warnings, but they come off as sermons laced with obscenities. I get a bad feeling when bouncers overreact and then give second chances. Unreasonable authority without definitive action invites defiance, or worse, revenge.

In-between sets I step around the roped off area and sit at the end of an empty hall to enjoy a beer in silence. It's where the motel complex offices are, and before long one of the doors opens and a man steps out. He's the owner, apparently, because a woman who appears to be in charge of security approaches him like an employee. The biggest security guard, who wears an earphone as if he were protecting the president from international terrorists, strides past me and faces them. "This fucking band is never coming back here again," he says to the man, and I start to pay attention.

"These fucking guys are egging the crowd on. They're making fun of security."

I look at the signboard behind me—two comedians and a dance band are playing next week. It occurs to me that nearly every bouncer here is part-time, that they've been rounded up for a one-time job because this venue doesn't routinely book acts that require more than two security guards.

"They win that bitch tee-vee thing, and we get to clean up all their shit," the security guard says, and then the three of them huddle like coaches at halftime.

Early in the second set, during "Guerilla Radio," Nick looks distracted, then halts his rap and says, "What the fuck" into the mike just as Tony stops scratching. "Hey, chill the fuck out," Nick shouts, and I step forward, but DJ Worm dives into the crowd, taking on one of the security goons who, I can see now, have laid out Butch.

Mark wrestles his bass over his head and jumps in, but two bouncers are holding Tony, and three others are wrestling Butch out the door. "Fuck this place," Nick yells. "We're out of here."

I watch Nick and Aaron and Chris to see if they're going to kamikaze into the struggle, but Nick holds the mike close to his mouth for a series of complaints punctuated by "Fuck this place," and Aaron lays his guitar onto the rack beside the other two he has on stage.

As I slip forward, Chris finally pushes back from his drum kit and follows Aaron down the steps by the side of the stage. There are stupid choices to be made; a half dozen bouncers have formed a semi-circle so near the stage that Nick's amplified taunts sound like a death wish. Aaron, when he uses just his natural voice to shout "Nice work" and "Way to fuck up the night" at the red shirts, nearly sounds like the voice of reason, but sure enough, the bouncers, suddenly, all face the stage, and Nick drops the microphone just as the owner steps up beside him. "These bouncers are fucked up," Nick says, but he follows the owner through the door behind Chris and Aaron, heading, I'm suddenly sure, to his office for a summit meeting. As the door closes, I hear Nick say to him, "This whole place is fucked up."

"What a bunch of morons," Aaron says, and then he turns toward a girl who looks, among this crowd, like she's dressed for church. He smiles and puts his arm around her. "This is Betty Jo," he says, as if she were one more blessing from the gods of rock and roll.

"We just had Easter dinner a couple of hours ago," Aaron says, "and now we're working for assholes." When Chris sighs like a quiz show loser, Betty Jo smiles again, relying on the weapon of good cheer.

"What now?" she says, and Aaron throws his palms out to either side.

Nick comes back. "They won't pay us unless we finish," he says. "Perfect," Aaron says.

Nick gives Betty Jo a hug, and then he turns to the rest of the band. "Let's rock and get the fuck out of here."

A minute later, the house lights dimmed again, the crowd, a mix of regulars and former table-sitters, bunches near the stage. Butch is in the front row now, and as soon as Nick says, "I want to see all you motherfuckers go crazy," the band launches into their cover of "Jump Around," the crowd rocking in a subdued way, waiting for the exhortation to "Jump. Jump. Jump. Everybody jump." And then the first ten rows leap almost in unison, leap again, shoulders slamming.

I move up through the crowd to focus on the band's anger. Aaron thrusts his guitar toward the crowd, his body all angles in a zigzag rhythm that screams "Fuck you" at the security guards three feet below him. Even as Nick roars an extended "Jumppppppppp" as the song closes, Aaron delivers the opening riff of "Bulls on Parade." The fans are smacking each other with forearms, those who aren't moshing driven back into me by the swirling crowd. The crowd screams the chorus: "Bulls on parade," thrusting their fists. As I look around, I notice two exit doors in the rear are open, and I can see state policemen filing into the lobby. The owner apparently panicked even before the band returned to the stage and called in the cops.

Suddenly, as the song ends, somebody appears onstage in a Michael Meyers mask. He paws at Nick in a slasher-movie mock attack, doing his best to make us recall the action in *Halloween*. The bouncers on either side of the stage are stone. The other bouncers are all farther from the mosh pit than I am. Ten seconds of horseplay, the crowd roaring, and then Nick says, "This is one of ours; you know what the fuck to do." Aaron cranks out the opening riff of "Heave," their most fist-pumping, crowd-frenzying original, and when the Michael Meyers imitator shoves Nick to the stage, Aaron repeats the riff, Nick springing up at last to roar, "So, get the fuck up," the masked man diving into the crowd, carried along by dozens of hands while the back doors open as if he's broken a light-sensor. Immediately, the state police, nine of them by my count, pour in. They pull the masked man down and tear off his mask to reveal a laughing Hyland.

The lights come up and the sound cuts off on stage. The band stands watching. I recognize John, the fan who's a prison guard, trying to help Hyland, and when he puts his hand on the shoulder of a state policeman, he gets maced for his trouble, wrestled down and dragged and billy-clubbed in the ribs before he's rolled over and handcuffed. For the second time in half an hour I walk toward the stage as if being near the band will prevent chaos.

"Whoa," Aaron is saying, "this is genuine bullshit."

By now there are a dozen fans on stage. The mikes are dead, but two of them are screaming in unison: "Fuck this place. Come to Scranton on Friday. You can go crazy there."

"I want to see what happened to John and Hyland," Aaron says, and the rest of the band follows, stopping in the lobby while he goes outside. The state police are bunched up on the sidewalk. They've taken their hats off, and I can see that seven of them have shaved heads. I think of the shaved heads of John and his prison guard buddies; the haircut seems part of their uniform. Every red-shirted bouncer but the two bald ones has a Marine haircut.

A woman screams an obscenity at the police. When she walks toward them, still taunting, two of them slam her face down on the asphalt and cuff her.

"That makes four of them we got," the head bouncer says, citing the number as if it were a body count.

"Make you proud," another woman spits at him.

He takes a step towards her and smiles like The Joker. I take a breath and consider choices, but he stops, listening through his earpiece, and goes back inside. I count six squad cars in the parking lot. It's as if they have cornered a hostage taker in the motel complex.

"What complete assholes these bouncers are," Aaron says to the fan, pitching his volume a tweak higher than conversation level.

She turns her palms down and gestures with the universal sign for *shut up*. "Don't get yourself fucked over by these goons," she says. "They have John in one of those cars, but Hyland's okay."

Aaron looks relieved. "Now I have to find Betty Jo," he says, and she nods. But when he tries the door, it's locked. From the other side of the glass a bouncer gives him a thumbs down. "I'm in the fucking band," Aaron shouts. "I have to get my equipment."

The bouncer shrugs, but then he opens the door, and I slip in behind Aaron before he reconsiders. I want to ask him if he's watched *Road House* and see if he gets it. "Betty Jo's upstairs," Nick says in the lobby, and Aaron jogs up a plush-carpeted staircase fit for Cinderella running from the ball.

Moments later, as the security manager looks on, Betty Jo and Aaron come downstairs. They're holding hands, but Aaron's right one is balled in a fist. The security woman turns toward my wife and me, pleased, it seems, to see two people her age. "You have a nice Easter?" she asks.

"Until the Gestapo ruined it," I say.

We hold each other's eyes. My wife puts her hand on my elbow, and then she steps between me and the security manager to shake the hand of one of the bald bouncers. "Thank you, sir," she says. "You're the only one who showed any common sense this evening."

He beams. "My name's Danny," he says, and I remember him crouched beside Aaron on the stage, how he kept his post through both disturbances. *The good guys,* I think, though the security woman is frowning in a way that makes me believe my wife has sacrificed Danny's job to make her point.

"Say it now, motherfucker. Say 'I'm gonna fuck shit up.'"
— Todd, a bouncer, Allentown

When the Allentown show ends and the band's equipment is packed, I step outside to chaos. I recognize two of the fans who were thrown out, and they've enlisted allies, come back to challenge the bouncers. It's a bad idea. They're taking their second beating of the night, saving face with a series of obscenities and stupid threats.

"You were told to stay the fuck out," the would-be professional wrestler screams at the revenge-seekers. "Stay the fuck out means stay the fuck out."

Such a perfect equation—it's as if any amount of crushed ribs and bruised biceps is insufficient without an obscene directive. I watch from the parking lot as a paddy wagon arrives. Three more belligerent drunks are being loaded for processing and fines. Another three are bunched together, sullenly waiting their turn. Suddenly, this all seems monotonous, and I'm embarrassed by my rapt attention when two women walk toward me, one of them saying to the other, "What if one of them brings a gun back?"

I slide into the car, looking up at them as they pass, and say, "Somebody must."

The Roof Is On Fire

"I was in a music store last week," Aaron says the first time I see him after the Allentown show, "and I saw a guitar case with Strangers With Candy stickers on it." I smile, but Aaron shakes his head. "The kid was taking guitar lessons at the store."

I remember Aaron going for lessons at the mall near our house, how he labored through one song at a time to gain a repertoire while I thought he was memorizing rather than learning. I was happy when he stopped after a few lessons because I thought the instructor was just a burnout who was willing, for fifteen dollars an hour, to listen to classic rock being mangled by a twelve-year-old boy with a new guitar.

"Here's the good part," Aaron says. "The instructor was teaching him 'Perfect.' I had him play a little, and then we sat down and ran through it together. His teacher had some of it wrong. It was cool and weird at the same time to be showing him a song I helped to write."

And now I remember that Aaron, after he stopped taking those lessons, started to rely on listening closely to tapes in order to teach himself, beginning with Metallica's *Ride the Lightning,* mastering exactly the songs he most enjoyed through hours of repetition.

"Here's something you'll get into," he says, sliding an official-looking certificate across the table toward me. It looks like a diploma, something to be framed, and sure enough, in the upper right-hand corner, is the seal of the city of Wilkes-Barre, Pennsylvania.

"Resolution," the document begins. "Whereas . . ."

The language has all the trappings of something that would be

73

read at a ceremony in the town square just prior to the Revolutionary War. "Now, Therefore Be It Resolved—"

Aaron smiles. "Who knows what they were thinking?" he says, and I read on, determined to finish every word of it.

" . . . hereby congratulates Strangers With Candy on being crowned MTV's Ultimate Cover Band and on the release of their CD 'No Need.' Introduced by Councilman . . ."

Underneath the proclamation is the signature of the City Clerk. A cover letter explains how the congratulatory councilman learned about the band from his daughter Kelly, who is a big fan.

I think of the guest books and the message boards on the fan sites that have sprung up like dandelions in the two months since the MTV show first aired. I fish out my own souvenirs, printed copies of the on-line dialogue:

If you saw them on MTV and thought they rocked—JUST WAIT!!!—that was just a tease. See them live. They are off the hook!!!! Their originals are soooo intense. You will sooooo feel their music in every fucking cell of your body!!! Plus, for real, what totally nice buncha guys . . . —Lysa

If any of you'd like to come to my room with me let me know —Sarah

You guyz are the fucking best thing that ever came out of this area—You are what northeast pa needed!!!! —gr8ful

You guys have a lot of talent and are VERY VERY VERY good looking! Drools—sorry, I'll control myself now —MB

U guys r fucking insane!!! Keep tearin shit up —Kyle

"That's enough," Aaron says. "You need to stop reading this stuff. I don't even own a computer."

"If you had won a book prize, you wouldn't have to worry about all this attention," I say, but Aaron doesn't smile.

The next night Aaron calls at 10:45. "Nikki's going to play our CD on The Bear some time after 11:00," he says.

"What's after 11:00 mean?"

"After 11:00."

It's an impasse. The Bear's radio tower is ten miles from where Aaron lives in Wilkes-Barre, but over eighty miles from where I live, and though it has a strong signal, the station doesn't come in even close to clearly inside the house. If I'm going to hear anything, I have to drive around in the car. How long can I cruise Selinsgrove with the radio on? Or simply sit in the driveway, thinking that a neighbor might believe I'm so stumbling drunk I can't remember how to open the car door?

I choose driving. At 10:55 I head out, stopping for gas so I feel useful. It's 10:59 when I start pumping, so I leave the radio on just in case "after 11:00" means "seconds after."

Sure enough, just as I'm screwing the gas cap back on, Nikki announces Strangers With Candy and their brand new CD *No Need*, and I sit down, leaving the door open, turning up the radio to party volume for "Key of Me," my favorite of the seven songs.

The guy at the next pump, walking back to his car from paying inside the Coastal Mart, eyes me, but for the next four minutes I'm ecstatic. And when, at 11:06, I get out to pay, I see the lights are dimmed inside.

"We close at 11:00," the woman at the counter says. "We were wondering what happened to you, whether we should call somebody."

"My son's band was on the radio," I say.

She looks at me. "Strangers With Candy?" she says, and the night turns perfect.

Despite Aaron's warning, I keep reading the message boards. Some are so long they read like short stories:

swc fucking kicked the shit— Butch announced them from on top of the speaker then jumped off and landed on my fucking head! I got my ass beat cuz I was up front then I was thrown over the railing it was the shit!! I got myself outta the pit and then I went back in for violence fetish and got thrown over the railing and the security dick grabbed my balls and unzippered my pants and shit so I went right back into the moshing area got a bloody nose scratches all over my goddamned back I lost my sneaker and my sweaty ass shirt got ripped off. All in all except for the bad air conditioning and the fact you didn't have room to move your hands around that show fucking rocked —bangin

Okay, I know you all were there. And so was I!!!! I got in again and today was my 18th birthday. It was the best show ever!!!! Nick is the cutest and I love him!!!! It was the best birthday ever—my friends paid for me to get in—one of them being NicksCandyGirl—hey honey!!!! Even had a few drinks, but it didn't matter cause I was there to see them and they kicked ass!!!! One thing that was funny that happened was this fat asshole in a wifebeater that was throwing his body around at everyone who didn't want to mosh. This one girl screamed at him and told him that if he didn't stop she was gonna kick him in the balls!!!! You go girl!!!! It was pretty funny but he was an asshole making everyone miserable!!!! He had to weigh over 200 lbs and he was throwing himself into small people and girls. That girl should have kicked him in the nuts!!!! That was the funniest thing that happened last night!!!! —Candy4Nick

And finally, in May, sitting inside a Wendy's halfway between my house and Aaron's apartment, I overhear my first outside-of-a-show conversation about the band, two young women who could, for all I know, have graduated from high school with my son five years before.

"I was like oh my god Strangers with Candy totally kick fucking ass," the thinnest and palest of the three anorexic-looking women says. "I was like who are they?"

"So I was like they are awesome the whole time they were on MTV. Their music was killer," the woman beside her says. All of them look as if they've forgotten they never come out in the daylight, that the cheese fries and Cokes each of them are swallowing might thicken their tiny waists.

The third one frowns. "I got in this huge fight with my friend about Strangers With Candy because he always tells me they suck and shit and I'm like 'fuck you.' It's annoying."

I want all three to keep talking. Thirty years ago or more I talked like this about Jimi Hendrix and Cream to friends just out of college who'd decided that great music had ended with the Temptations and the Four Tops. "Like I can totally feel it when Nick sings," the second one says, drifting into platitude.

"They're not a cover band just cause they won," the thinnest one declares. "They don't sound like one band. They don't even kinda sound like one band. They are their own band."

The third woman shakes her head. "It's not just my one friend. Most of my friends don't care."

The second woman sits up and waves a cheese-soaked French fry. "Get new friends," she says. "Those ones suck."

"Suck for real," the third woman says.

"For sure, they suck," the first says, making it unanimous.

"You should have been hanging with us last week," Aaron says. "We turned down a contract offer."

In late May the buzz is still going about Strangers With Candy, but I know they haven't officially showcased for anybody yet. "These guys invited us to their apartment after the show. They said they had a record company, and they thought we were the shit. It sounded shady, but we weren't going anywhere, and they were hosting, so we went."

Aaron laughs. "You'll like this," he says. "We get to their place, and the first thing they say when we get inside is, 'Congratulations, you're signed. You're our first act.' It was like they were reading their speech from one of those Publishers Clearing House envelopes."

I don't know what to say, but Aaron doesn't need prompting. "'You guys are set. You don't have to worry about anything,' they said. We were like 'What's up with these dudes?' They were both younger than we are."

Aaron's right. I love these stories, the ones that are funny without consequences, and he goes on without waiting for me to ask a question. "But here's the best part," he says. "They had a sign up on the wall for their record company, and it was made out of a piece of cardboard that was cut out of an old box or something. You know, it was obviously once a box. Homemade like that, and everything printed with a magic marker. They had a skull and crossbones logo, like they were Poison Records or something. It was hilarious. Every time I looked at it I had to make myself stop staring."

"So you were out of there?" I finally ask.

"No, that's what's weird. We hung out half the night. After that, they didn't say another word about signing us. We just drank their beer."

"Dumb and Dumber, record executives."

"Exactly."

I sit back, smiling, but Aaron turns serious. "Dad," he says, "we're going to get signed. And soon. Atlantic's interested. Universal. There's no doubt this is going to happen."

In June my wife and I watch the news from New York like always, keeping in touch with the city our daughter has moved to. This Sunday night a reporter airs a story about a police raid of the twelve-hour Eden Rave in New Jersey.

"Music and drugs," the reporter says, summing up my sense of what a rave is all about. "And this time," she goes on, "public nudity as well." An amateur video comes on, three girls dancing topless to electronic music, then two others, then another, whoever was holding that camera targeting bare breasts that are now being blurred for the sake of the New York City television news.

The story is a lengthy one, the police are interviewed about the multiple drug arrests. The report turns into a feature that includes a brief background report on the history and nature of raves, the short documentary concentrating on their heavy association with drugs. Just before the report ends, the program for the Eden Rave comes up on the screen and there, at the very top and in the center: Strangers With Candy. The picture of the program disappears so quickly I think I'm hallucinating, but my wife says, "See that?" and the sighting is confirmed.

If I still have doubts, the next day's fan sites corroborate the news.

> I saw you guys at that rave called Eden—I was walking around in this techno stuff then I heard you guys in another room—it was fuck awesome —Rich

Days later, that show is at the top of my list of queries when we visit Aaron, but before I can ask about it he shows Liz and me the program, and I feel, staring at the band's name at the top of the page, as if I have physical confirmation of my very first UFO. "We saw this on the news," I say.

"That's what people keep telling us," Aaron says, "but we did our thing, packed up, and left. We missed all the topless girls."

"You didn't see anything going on?"

"When we were leaving, we saw police cars pulling in. We didn't stay to investigate—we had another booking."

The program features a computer-generated Adam and a voluptuous, naked Eve on the cover, leaves swirling up their legs and ending strategically at their waists.

"We are bringing together the forces of the heavens and the earth to provide you with the most beautiful and euphoric party atmosphere ever created," the pamphlet proclaims. All of the copy is done in illuminated letters, script reminiscent of medieval monks lettering a translation of the New Testament by hand.

An Adam and Eve contest is promoted. A best body contest with contestants wearing "little leaf gear."

Strangers With Candy, the program reminds, is playing "In the Garden." I think of bare-chested Adams and Eves. The promo paragraph nearly shouts: "Two words: Blowin' Up! On-point blend of dope singing and screaming stage voice mixed with a bangin' stage presence will have you ladies fallin' in love and all you hard rocks getting roused in the pit."

Surprisingly, on a program that features descriptions of twelve hours of techno music, Tony gets a boost of his own as a deejay. "Break it down with his ill skillz," the copy reads. "Partaay!"

I sound out that call to arms just loud enough to make Aaron say, "Stop it, Dad."

Three weeks later, the message from Aaron on the answering machine is short and clear: "Your son is now a member of a signed band." And that's it, all my wife and I know for twenty-four hours because there's no question the band's first-day celebration doesn't include extended conversations with parents.

"It was cool," he says the next afternoon. "Everybody was psyched. We're on the same label as Godsmack, Dad. Monte Lipman came in when we were doing the paperwork."

"Okay," I say, a vague signal that I need to know why Monte Lipman is important.

"Monte Lipman's the president of Universal, Dad. He actually came to our show to personally sign us. That's got to help. It makes us a priority."

Later in the week we see pictures in the Wilkes-Barre newspaper, an article about the signing. There's no question their local celebrity has taken on the weight of money now. Aaron laughs off my questions about the band's celebration. "Nothing much," he says. "The only stupid thing was we went into this bar in Manhattan, and Nick did some Jager shots, and then when we came outside he puked on the sidewalk. Just kind of stupid, really."

By the end of July I've told the band I'm writing about them. I print out the twenty pages of description of early shows and they all read it. "We're good with this," they agree, but when I sit backstage and try to interview them, they somehow change.

Though they talk without hesitation, only Nick seems natural when he answers questions. "I had hair all over the place when I was in my first band," he says. "My mom would drive me to the bars and drop me off, then I'd go in to sing and play. She was good with it, but I was only thirteen when I started, and the other guys in the band were old, you know, twenty years older than any of us are now. It was fucked up and great at the same time."

The rest of the band sounds like they do in the published interviews I've read in local magazines and newspapers. Tony, who never stops talking in street slang, suddenly says things like "I was a drummer, and when I bought all the equipment I need for performing, my parents asked, 'What's a DJ? What do you do in this band?'"

Chris, always more quiet than the others, is even briefer and less helpful: "My parents thought it was just a phase," he says, and when I wait for him to elaborate, our corner of the dressing room swells with silence while he looks past me as if he's completed a recital of the encyclopedia of interview answers.

I decide that what I need to do is disappear, even from my son, in order to really hear and see the band. And so I stop asking them questions, slump into whatever ratty chair is available backstage, and hold a beer, doing my best imitation of a dozing fan during a half dozen shows in the three months left between their being signed by Universal and their going off to Massachusetts to record their first CD for national release.

The second night I try to interview by not asking questions, and an hour before the show Tony starts in on remembering a job he had selling knives. "A thousand dollars for one knife," he says. "I'm thinking right on with this, get that kit together and go out to make my fortune."

Even though he's overpricing, I remember a student of mine, recently graduated, who settled in my office years ago with those knives so expensive I wondered out loud to him if he expected to ever sell even one set. "No," he said, "but if I do, I'll make a lot of money."

That student told me a year later that he sold one set altogether. "To my parents," he admitted, laughing because by then he'd gotten a "real" job at a regional magazine, but Tony, apparently, sold none.

"Two weeks of zero," he says. "Nobody in my neighborhood needed a knife to like cut through bone and shit."

"Bad jobs?" Aaron says, "The one that sucked the most was washing dishes in this restaurant. I lasted exactly two days." I remember the restaurant, how Aaron quit because of the manager's verbal abuse, how I'd felt justified in telling people not to eat dinner there after the owner refused to cut Aaron a check for the time he'd worked. I want to break in to triumphantly declare that the restaurant Aaron is bad-mouthing has gone out of business, but Nick gets started about working at a Heinz pet food factory.

"Fucking worst," he says, "I was going out every night with that stink still on me. It was the worst. And every morning I'd drag my ass in to work all hung over, and half the time the smell of all that cheap meat made me throw up on the floor."

The Worst of Everything—it's a topic that comes up so often it feels like a spell that's cast against a bad performance. "Remember that night in State College?" Mark says. "The crowd expected a Top 40 band and kept yelling for 'Jessie's Girl'? We got booed all night, and then Nick yelled 'How many people here totally hate our guts? Please clap.' And they did."

"Long and loud," Aaron says.

Or the Best of Everything—the stories that get spun out after shows, Mark retelling how Nick had a coverall workman's suit on for an early show, and it was so hot on stage that he took the top half off and tied it around his waist. And how, after jumping around for a few minutes, he looked down and saw that "Little Nick" had come out.

Jim Morrison with a sense of humor, I think, and then I remember I'm thirty years older than these guys, that the girls pushing into the dressing room all have their backs to me, and I shake hands and start the ninety minute drive on the deserted roads of 3 A.M. The stories are so quirky that I'm not surprised when most of them show up in an on-line interview. Who wouldn't want to listen? And which of them would remember he'd told that story before?

And now I mix with the crowd at every show. I've seen enough moshing and stage diving to make chaos seem routine, but aside from Butch and Hyland and a handful of other regulars, I haven't heard voices firsthand, so I listen to conversations during breaks instead of heading back to the dressing room.

All I have to do is lean against the bar and sip from a glass bottle like the hundreds of others that seem to roll underfoot. "Their music is so killer, and last time it was like about 110 degrees but that made it all sweaty good when people went fucking nuts, and then that bounce did a hose on the pit and shit and it was all good."

These snippets seem like the Flash Stories that trendy magazines feature, one-minute or less of monologue before the storytellers drift away or concentrate on drinking. "I couldn't believe Nick's wearing it. My boyfriend and I were shopping last week, and I seen this shirt, and I said this is something Nick would wear, and my boyfriend bought it for him. He said Nick was really cool about it and shook his hand and gave him a hug, and here he is with the shirt on and getting it all sweaty and shit, and it's like from us."

I loiter on the floor for a few minutes after the shows, the stories even shorter now that everybody is being herded toward an exit: "I was in the very front against the barricade and got kicked in the head a few times and almost broke my arm—it was completely worth it."

"The fuckers that were fighting pissed me off real bad—other than that it was a neat show."

"I had a great time except for the fucking bruise I'm getting on my right breast from some stupid whore in a black shirt."

I pay special attention when I hear my son's name: "I was right up front near Aaron. He's my fave."

"God yes. He can live with me and be my sex toy. He'd never want to leave the house."

"I want to run right up and tell him I'd be happy to go home with him. Whatever makes him happy would make me happy. You don't mess with perfection."

"You shouldn't watch these videos, Dad. You'll be disappointed," Aaron says, when he hands over a set of tapes because, I tell him, "I want to see everything."

"That's never a good idea," he adds.

"I've never lasted past 3 A.M. Nobody would want me there then, even if I could handle it."

"That's when the stupid shit happens, that's for sure."

The videos aren't as bad as I expected. Nobody seems to be doing drugs. Nobody is proposing sex acts on camera. Nobody is being abused or humiliated.

I understand I've set my expectations so low I'm pleased when it's just excessive drinking, sexual promises, and routine profanity. And Aaron, for the most part, is on the fringe of everything. He appears to have my habits, enjoying being there, but more a voyeur than a participant.

It's Nick who volunteers to throw up on cue for the camera. And it's Nick who tells sex-laced stories for the young women who hang on every word. He's a nonstop front man, what every band needs. Charisma. Balls. He nearly glows with the joy of strutting. All Aaron has to do is hang back and be the guitarist, celebrity by association.

But by late summer, when I go back to the fan sites, the tone occasionally changes: "What's with all these ex-girlfriends of the band members coming in here and bringing up the past all of a sudden?" asks swcrocksmysocks.

Predictably, a virtual cat fight begins.

"Jealous much?" types nicksoldflame, and the messages scroll down through accusations and slurs and guesswork about identities and truthfulness until a trio of rebuttals comes rapid-fire:

"So you feel like being a bitter, pushy bitch that shoves things in other people's faces. None of us are jealous of you. This whole thing is pathetic."

"There's a reason why you're his EX."

"Did he go down on you the first time you went out with him?"

Fortunately, there's still a silliness about their fame that alleviates this surfacing anger. There's a Butch look-a-like now. He's managed the spiked blond hair just right, the choke collar, the leather jacket. What this fan of a fan hasn't given up, somehow, is his mustache, as if it's his own signature. I almost wish for an Aaron's father look-a-like, some fiftyish man wearing a soft-collar shirt and eavesdropping.

But late in the summer, the band rumored to be leaving soon to record their national CD, a persistent ugliness creeps into the Internet discussions. Backlash. A cluster of messages about how Strangers With Candy sucks. And when the name change to Driver is officially announced, avoiding a lawsuit by the Comedy Central television show, the messages simply add, "They suck no matter what their name is. They sold out for MTV. They sound like clones of Limp Bizkit."

The messages come from what seems like the inevitability of resentment that arrives with every highly publicized success. Those who feel left behind look for the worst in the successful. They complain and whine and seethe with anger because as soon as the band isn't "theirs" anymore, their role in the local cult diminishes to bystanding and repeating stories about how they were "there" when nobody cared and how the band has "changed."

Even worse, though, are the stalkers and the in-person trash talkers. The band travels much less now. *Good,* I think at first, until their celebrity in Wilkes-Barre introduces problems not confined to the Internet.

There's a woman who finds Aaron's apartment and drives around and around and around in her red car, the ruined muffler emitting a distinctive rumble that he and Betty Jo, who lives with him now, can identify when she's a block away. One or two nights of this might be good for Aaron's ego, I think, remembering the teenage girls who slid flowers under the windshield wipers of the car Aaron drove when he was sixteen and played in Seed. I was pleased, happy for him even though he didn't act as if he welcomed such attention. But it's not long before the stalker's boyfriend believes Aaron seeks her out rather than it being the other way around.

"He wants to kick my ass," Aaron says. "Who would he believe? His crazy girlfriend or me?"

He starts to lecture me about my enthusiasm for his celebrity. Earlier in the summer, at a show at a local college, I'd been so taken with the joy of a group of thirteen-year-olds who'd picked up paper bags so the band would have something to sign, that I'd told them I could get Aaron to sign the red Strangers With Candy shirts all three of them were wearing. "Aaron's dad," they chimed. "that's so cool." And for a few minutes they beamed at me as if I was holding a guitar, squirming with delight when Aaron scrawled his name across their backs with magic marker.

One of those girls had found my e-mail address because I'd told her where I worked. And after I answered her first message, she'd bombarded me with questions.

Finally, she'd sent me a handwritten personal letter full of questions about Aaron, and I didn't need my son to remind me, as he did when I told him, "That's not cool."

"You can't be friendly, not like that," Aaron said at the time, and now, as if he thinks I'm still capable of goofy naïveté, he says, "I walked out of my apartment this week and there were two girls standing in the yard. Just standing there. They just stared at me. What were they doing before I came out? Who tells them where I live?"

I think of all those girls who fill the web site with narratives of desire that seem to be squealed rather than written. I keep to myself that before I decided to stop I gave out his phone number to the first two girls who called my house. "People go through my garbage," he says.

"I have Aaron's pizza crusts," I say, doing my best mimic of a message board. "I own three of his used Coke cans."

Aaron grimaces. For a moment it seems entirely plausible that I might be quoting something I've actually read.

The week that school begins I drive to Wilkes-Barre for an early show. Driver is playing for another college's freshman orientation, hundreds of eighteen-year-olds, most of whom have never heard of Strangers With Candy, let alone the band by their new name Driver.

I walk by the amateur security, students dressed in blue shirts who look at me anxiously, wishing that I would stop instead of barring my way. I glance at a blond guy to my left, and when I see Mark and Chris sitting in chairs inside what looks, from all of the props, to be the student-theater dressing room, I say, "Where's Aaron?"

"Aaron?" Mark says. "He's out somewhere."

"Huh?" I hear from just to my left, and Mark laughs when I look again and discover my son, now blond and nose-pierced. "You're so observant," Aaron says.

"Blond means somebody else's family," I say. "I guess this is new." I hand him three videotapes of old shows I've borrowed. The nose ring makes me think of the party scene in one, dark-haired Aaron laughing at 3 A.M. in the parking lot of some club in New Jersey.

"Just today," he says. "Why not?" he adds, anticipating a question.

An hour later, on stage, Aaron looks like somebody I don't know. It's as if I'm watching a band with which I have no emotional connection, and I'm uneasy with how easily I become detached. One nose ring and a dye job, and my son looks like a guy who would make me smirk to myself when I passed him on the street.

I examine the crowd, evaluating how a room full of college students reacts to Driver. The band has stopped playing covers, so only the Strangers With Candy fans have ever heard any of the songs before. Within three songs I sense things going wrong.

The mosh pit is discouraged, not by the amateur security staff, but by disinterest. Butch and a few regulars, who have slipped by the security as easily as I have, look lost with nothing to do but listen.

Worse, before the band plays "Swallow" they play a taped excerpt from *Gummo,* an old cult movie, a scene where a young girl talks about being molested. The students look so uncomfortable they seem to be growing younger, and some drift away. The song itself speeds the exodus, Nick singing, "Do you spit, do you swallow?" the sexual connotation unmistakable.

Half the room is gone by the end of the song. Forty-five minutes into the seventy-five-minute show, there are only thirty people left, and I recognize fifteen of them. I watch the band look at each other, and a moment later they launch into "Heave"—"So get the fuck up," Nick roars, his call to chaos traveling unimpeded to the back wall. In the nearly empty room the song sounds crude and stupid, the kind of anthem you'd love if your goal in life was to be drunk every minute. "Thanks," Nick says at the end, and all five of them are off stage before the diehards can politely clap.

"Fuck this," Nick says backstage.

"Double that," Aaron says as he discovers the videotapes I've returned to him have been stolen.

I keep my VOW of "no more contact," but in the early fall, when Aaron comes home for what might be a last full-family get-together, I ask if he wants to see all the posts about "Aaron's new look."

"What do you mean, 'Aaron's new look?'" he says.

"It's all over the new Driver web site. There were pictures two days after the college disaster."

"Somebody posted a picture of me looking like this in two days?"

"And they're already copied. There's more than one new fan site for Driver."

I show Aaron the new sites. Because he doesn't own a computer, he's never even seen the old Strangers With Candy sites, so every girl or woman who's fantasized about him in public has gone unnoticed.

Wow, Aaron is amazing. I have to be honest, I liked the black hair better. He doesn't need to change. He is perfect the way he is. Even with the new hair and the nose ring, I couldn't keep my eyes off him. Oh God I want to touch him. I'm sorry, I know I'm obsessed, but can you blame me? God I bet he's good in bed!

He's more anxious than interested as he reads. "This celebrity stuff wears out fast, Dad," he says. "It's not just somebody crazy like the woman who drives around the block. We're well-known enough now that boyfriends and husbands are pissed at us just because we are who we are."

This time I just listen. He's way ahead of me on this subject. Any wishful thinking I've ever done about women attracted to me because of my writing has remained just that. "I'm not making this up," Aaron says. "These women say shit to us all the time, and then they're drunk and say it to each other and their boyfriends hear it and get pissed and want to kick our asses and fuck us up."

What he finally tells me is that it's already happened. He was out the week before at a local club, and as usual there were a few men who cast threatening glances. The story seems muddled. Aaron doesn't elaborate on any of the characters. But even though I don't understand the motivation, I'm transfixed by the outcome.

Aaron and Tony had been sitting with Mark and his girlfriend, Laura. Looks had been exchanged with a small group of men. Eventually, when only Mark was sitting at the bar, his girlfriend in the bathroom, Aaron and Tony at a pool table, one of those men approached and, without speaking, put his hands to Mark's throat and choked him.

"We saw what was up," Aaron said. "It got crazy fast. Mark grabbed a bottle and broke it over the guy's face, lacerated him. There was so much blood it was like Carrie at the prom."

"This is a genuine bad guy," Aaron goes on. "We found out later he hadn't shown up for his arraignment that day on other shit he was into. We were happy as hell to have the police show up, but he was majorly pissed."

I start to imagine guns and knives, but Aaron isn't through. "There was more craziness," he says. "The police were doing their thing outside, and I looked down the hall that goes to the parking lot to see what was up, and this other guy spotted me and gave me a look so I turned around and went back inside, and then that guy, from out of nowhere, runs up behind me and thumps me in the back of the head with his fist. I went down, Dad. I was all dizzy and disoriented. There was even blood. I thought I'd got hit with a bottle, and then he ran back outside. They'll find us again. They'll mess up our van or our equipment or us if they get the chance. That guy that Mark cut—he'll look in the mirror and be pissed every day. He'll be back, count on it. The cops want Mark and me to press charges. No way. Everybody knows where I live and what I do. They can read in the papers where I'll be."

For the first time, I wish him back in college, a traditional music major who will study the history of the guitar instead of play one. Disappointments with bookings, shows that went sour, money problems with club owners all seem suddenly trivial.

"You'll travel soon," I say. "Another month and you won't be so visible."

"Not here, but if we get big, it'll be the same bullshit everywhere we go. I hear stories almost every day about paternity suits, assault charges. There are people who think it's a job to get money from celebrities."

He sits across from me in my living room. Blond. The nose ring. Multiple ear piercings. But this second time confronting his "new look" I already don't pay any attention. I see how thin he is. I sound like my mother when I tell him to eat more; I pour orange juice in a glass and tell him to drink some before he starts on the Pepsi. The last thing I worry about is whether or not he looks more and more like somebody in a teenage girl's fantasy of a rock and roll band.

Signed

Within weeks of signing with Universal and changing its name, Driver goes to Philadelphia to record for a compilation CD. *Take a Bite Outta Rhyme* it's called, rock groups redoing well-known rap songs. Driver does Grandmaster Flash's "White Lines," a cautionary tale about the dangers of cocaine abuse. I get to hear it immediately because Aaron and Nick show up at my house around midnight the day after they record, CD copy in hand.

My wife is asleep, but the stereo is in the basement, and hearing the song is irresistible. "Just keep the volume reasonable," I say, and Aaron nods, but his opening riff bursts out louder than I've ever set the volume for.

"Whoa," I say, and then I give in, listening like a father trying to make out his child's first word. There's no question Nick has been drinking, and though I want to give my son the benefit of the doubt, he's wearing the enormous smile of a six pack on his face.

Nick cups his hand into a karaoke mike and works himself into a stage act, throwing himself into a just-audible lip synch. The song sounds raw and unpolished. *Primal,* I think, and then turn off that sort of pretentiousness, letting Aaron crank it up again, this time even louder. Their first national release is a moment that shouldn't be turned down. Driver will be on a CD with Sevendust, Staind, and The Bloodhound Gang. The rap metal genre is enormously popular; I imagine hundreds of thousands of sixteen-year-old white boys hearing a closer-to-the-suburban-bone version of urban toughness.

Three times I absorb every note, and then I listen to Aaron and

Nick tell me about the studio they recorded in, how the walls are lined with gold and platinum records. "This dude's connected," Nick says. "He's the shit."

"Phil Niccolo," Aaron says. "He's one of the Butcher Brothers, the guys who started Rough House Records. They did Cypress Hill. They did 311."

"Everybody," Nick agrees.

But when I hold to my limit of listening three times, they disappear to find people who think 1 A.M. is early. My wife sleeps through the whole thing, a night burglar's dream.

In the morning I'm up at 7 A.M. to open the side door after I hear a knock. Nick is standing in the doorway, Ben behind him. "Aaron said you'd be up," Nick says. "Sorry, we brought some shit here last night and forgot to take it with us."

"Sure," I say, a kind of one-size-fits-all answer.

Nick goes upstairs and within seconds comes back down with a paper bag that, this early in the morning, makes me peg it as a poor man's suitcase. "Thanks," he says, crossing the kitchen toward the door.

"No problem," I say. "Anyway, you're in the newspaper this morning, so maybe you want to take a look."

"Really?" Nick says, and I hand him the entertainment section, a picture of the band and an article about them being signed.

"The Selinsgrove connection," I say. "You're local heroes."

Nick holds on to the bag while Ben spreads the paper across the kitchen table, the two of them reading the article like generals examining a map of a battlefield. "We have to buy one of these," Nick says, and then he thanks me again. Ben just keeps a smile on, never saying a word, not even when they leave a moment later.

When Aaron shows up again in the middle of the afternoon I tell him I was surprised Nick and Ben would be up so early after celebrating. Aaron shrugs. "Dad," he says, "they were still going. They just needed more beer. What did you think was in the bag?"

I think of the two of them sitting somewhere with a beer in their hands at 8 A.M. I think of them on a front porch, waving good naturedly to families off to church. What I can't imagine is the two of them stopping to buy a Sunday newspaper.

The next time I hear "White Lines" Driver is the third band in a four-band lineup at Tink's that starts with Boiler Room and Isle of Que before it ends with Disturbed, the fast-breaking national act that headlines. The band room, when I walk in after Boiler Room's set, is chaos, women settled in on the couches among three bands. I hold a beer and wonder out loud if Disturbed will walk in, but Aaron shakes his head. "They're stars," he says, as if that explains everything.

I check the room more closely than I usually do because Isle of Que has two members who attended Susquehanna University. I recognize the one who was in a class of mine so long ago I know he's over thirty now. When I introduce myself, he smiles. When I tell him he was in my fiction writing class, he says, "Did I fail?"

"No," I say, but I remember his C– grade exactly, not a failure, but the lowest grade in the class that semester. And when, fifteen minutes later, I move onto the balcony to watch their show, I can hear and see at once that their performance will go unappreciated. There's no DJ; there's no drop-D-tuning on their guitars. All of them, in their early thirties and dressed in flannel and jeans like guys in a rural bar, look older than anyone on the floor below me. I'm not surprised when, after two songs, the catcalls and insults begin. "Get off the stage," I hear. "You suck" is repeated as a group chant. And finally, after four songs, the roar settles into "We want Strangers. We want Strangers. We want Strangers" as if the crowd's loyalties are built into the original name; nobody seems to be screaming for Driver.

Standing there, leaning on the balcony railing, I think of how I've seen both other signed bands with ties to Selinsgrove within the past month, and of how both those sightings have been depressing. I've watched the Badlees play to a crowd of less than a hundred at a free outdoor show, and here is Isle of Que playing to a full house that yells obscenities when they're not demanding that they get off the stage before their set is half over.

Worse, Aaron tells me when I go back into the dressing room, Isle of Que will likely be dropped. "They're our label-mates," he says. "They're on Universal, too, but not for long." I've heard two of their songs on the radio; The Badlees, I know, produce their own CDs now, years removed from selling nearly 200,000 copies of their national release and charting two singles. Driver is so new to this business they believe their music will be irresistible. And so do I, my uneasiness swept away a half hour later by the thunderous welcome for the band, every person in the club, as far as I can tell, pushing forward when the opening riff of "My Room" bursts from the amplifiers.

Once I have a CD copy of "White Lines" I'm determined to find somebody to play it for. I try the other three members of my weekly golf foursome, colleagues my age or older. I swing open the doors of my Celica in the parking lot just off the eighteenth green so the sound can carry to my obligated audience. Thirty seconds into the song two of my friends have backed up a few steps, but one moves forward, an encouraging sign. "That's something," one of the backsteppers says when the song ends.

The closest of the three says, "I have a fourteen-year-old son. I'll tell him to look for it on the Internet."

I try Tom, my friend who watched the MTV cover band show with me. Fifteen years younger than I am, he remembers the original, even before I slide the CD into the Celica's player. When it ends, Tom says "Turn it up," and we listen a second, and then a third time at teenage-cruising volume.

And then, a week later, Tom turns it up even louder as I drive him and two other colleagues in my van, riding through State College after a six-beer, three-bar faculty night out during a university retreat. Anybody within two blocks could hear "White Lines" by Driver, and when it ends the van holds the sort of silence that comes after a long sermon, one that's accompanied by a shuffling in the pews.

"Hmmm," one colleague finally says.

"Oh my," the other adds, exactly mimicking the reaction of the English Department secretary when she watched thirty seconds of the MTV Ultimate Cover Band contest.

Tom pushes the Play and Volume buttons, and Driver roars out of the speakers again, this time even louder. There are just enough miles before we reach the motel complex for the song to finish a second run, but not enough time for my other two colleagues to feel obligated to speak again.

The last show before the band goes to Massachusetts to record is at Cousin's in Hazleton. The room where they play is upstairs. Plan 9 is opening, something I've seen them do half a dozen times now, yet it's still odd watching Ben perform with other musicians. And then, near the end of the set, Ben says, "Thanks. We are Breaking Benjamin," reclaiming the name, and I think of the Breaking Benjamin sticker that's still on the side of the refrigerator in my kitchen, the sticker that's still on the back of the old blue van that carried Strangers With Candy, the sticker that's still on the mailbox just outside of the bank in Selinsgrove because Derek, two years ago now, stuck it there.

When they finish, Derek and I go backstage, both of us congratulating them on a good show. Jeremy seems so quiet and reserved it's as if he's joined a sort of National Honor Society for rock drummers, one that rewards good behavior.

The bass player, for the third time since I first saw this band, is different, and it makes me think of Hoover and the early months. I wonder how all of these temporary band members react to being fired. Chris was the one who'd broken the news to Hoover, waiting two weeks and several clandestine rehearsals with Mark before accounting for what must have seemed like a long lull to Hoover. "He seemed pissed but cool with it," Chris said, "but later, you know, he told me for a while he thought about killing everybody in the band."

I think *bravado* and *face-saving*, but Hoover is the guy who brought a gun to every show, and Aaron has told me he kept a closet full of weapons—an automatic rifle, a pistol, a machete, throwing stars. "At least that was at home," Aaron said the evening we sat outside on the deck right after the band had been signed, "but I remember when he started showing that stuff around. I told him to keep that shit closed up someplace."

For the second time since I'd been following the band I asked my son why a bass player would carry a gun to a show. "In case there was trouble. He didn't take any shit. He backed us up, I'll give him that. When that drunk pissed on our equipment in Dallas, he was in his face. Whenever anybody harassed us, he was the first to stand up and be counted. He wasn't afraid of anybody."

Now Nick starts telling us he's been robbed, that "some fucker who says he's my friend because that's the only people who have been in my house" has emptied the safe he keeps downstairs. I think of the advance from Universal, how much money that would be if Nick actually kept it all in his house like a recluse.

"He has to be goofing with us," Derek says to me undercover of the aggressive rock music being blasted through the club between acts. "He knows I've seen that safe, but there's no way he got robbed, or he'd be out with a posse."

The room goes quiet, as if everybody is mulling over the consequences of ill-chosen friendships and leaving a safe wide open during a party. "That fucker," Nick says again, and then he pulls the tab on a Yuengling Lager, leaving the rest of us to try conversation we can understand.

"You know where Nick lives?" Derek says as we cross the stage to rejoin the audience. "By the nuclear plant. Check it out some time. The road to his house is right there where the cooling towers sit."

"Homer Simpson," I say. And then I try to imagine standing in your yard and staring across a field to where those enormous towers rear up out of the landscape. How you might stuff the most money you've ever seen into a safe. How you might equate seeing that safe in your basement with having that money.

By now the place is packed, and except for a handful of diehard baseball fans who linger at the bar to watch the World Series, everybody has worked their way forward into a shoulder-to-shoulder mass. The mosh pit forms as soon as "My Room" begins. The fans that are here all know this is their last opportunity to see Driver until 2001; any bruises they receive tonight will be healed long before they have another shot at smashing into each other in front of the band.

When, visibly drunk, he lurches offstage after "Heave" finishes the chaotic set, Nick takes the mike backstage and lets the audience listen to him take a long, powerful piss. The room roars an approval, and an incoherent but rejuvenated Nick swaggers onto the stage as Aaron rips off a series of power chords. "This will be on *Take a Bite Outta Rhyme.* Check this shit out," Nick shouts, and the room surges forward for this encore, the mosh pit reforming for "White Lines," the club so electric with joy that Driver sounds like the next big thing just before they're off to Massachusetts to record.

"Alex Lifeson," Aaron answers, when I ask him, during the preproduction sessions he says they're having at their rehearsal space in Wilkes-Barre, who's producing the CD. He waits for a moment. "You don't know who that is, do you?" he adds.

"No idea."

"He's the guitarist for Rush." For once, Aaron seems starstruck, so I know Alex Lifeson has passed some kind of test as both a musician and a person. "He gave me a guitar, Dad. He brought it along for me. An acoustic. He's been listening nonstop to our demos, and he hands me that guitar right after he gets here."

"Good," I offer.

"Mark's changing his name for the CD," Aaron suddenly says. "He's Mark James now."

"Rock and roll," I say, imagining him abandoning Klepaski, his given name, like an unwanted baby.

"James is his middle name, so it's nothing big."

"It's his call."

"I'm thinking of changing my name, too." I feel my indifference switch to surprise. "I just wanted you to know ahead of time," Aaron goes on. "It's not like I'm changing it. Just the spelling."

He tells me it's going to be Fink instead of Fincke. "I got tired of people saying it wrong. Finkee. Finch. What the hell? Can't people read? Where's the H? The worst is Finkle. Where's the L? Every time I've done an interview I have to spend the first minute talking about my name. Now it's Fink and nobody can screw it up."

There's more revelation to come. The day after the preproduction sessions end, Aaron and Betty Jo invite Liz and Derek and me to dinner, announcing, as we finish an enormous serving of nachos at a Mexican restaurant midway between Wilkes-Barre and Selinsgrove, that they have "some news." Aaron pauses for a moment, looks at Betty Jo, and says, "You're going to be grandparents."

Only one extra beat goes by before Liz smiles and says "Congratulations." Because she's broken the ice, I get off easy, raising my beer in an unmistakable toast signal, clicking my bottle against Aaron's and Derek's before I touch the Pepsi-filled glass Betty Jo extends.

The band leaves for Massachusetts in two days. We spend another two hours talking around that table about everything but music. And when we get in the car to drive home Liz says at once, "I knew what was up as soon as I heard Betty Jo order a Pepsi."

"Really?" I say.

"Yes. She's taking care of herself now. I was happy to see that. For somebody who writes, you're so unobservant."

"I notice what's important," I begin.

"No, you don't."

Driver is recording at Longview Farms. Aaron calls to tell me, "It's way out in the sticks in some place called North Brookfield."

"I've been there," I say at once.

"Are you sure?" he says. "Why?"

"You remember when we went to visit my friend from college and you rode his daughter's horse?"

"I was like eleven or something."

"They live in West Brookfield. It's five miles away or something like that. I've been there four or five times since then, and we ate breakfast in North Brookfield a couple of times."

I don't bore him with my college reunion stories, or worse, sports-related trivia, but it's hard not to tell him my old friend has taken me to breakfast in North Brookfield because Mario Lemieux's uncle ran a small restaurant there.

That uncle, I know, has recently died, but I remember him showing us snapshots of Mario Lemieux celebrating with the Stanley Cup, candid photos from family gatherings, the kinds of pictures a man would take out only for close friends and relatives unless every photo included Mario Lemieux and he thought hockey was the most important thing a man could excel at.

That restaurant was small and quaint and unassuming, the way the rest of the town appears, which is part of Universal's plan for the band. Bring them here where there are few distractions, set them down in the Massachusetts version of the middle of nowhere, and trust the location will keep trouble to a minimum. After all, it's worked in the past. Aerosmith has recorded here. The Rolling Stones. Creed. Sevendust. I think of the members of those bands wandering into that restaurant, whether or not Mario Lemieux's uncle would have spread those snapshots across the counter for Mick Jagger or Steven Tyler.

And, according to Aaron, the system works for the first few days, though the method for recording is full of opportunities for the kind of restlessness that will test North Brookfield's ability to muffle trouble.

I learn that the drum tracks are laid down first when the CD is recorded. That the rest of the band has nothing to do for several days but wait their turn while Chris hammers out his parts over and over until Alex Lifeson thinks they're right on.

And then it's Mark's turn to lay down the bass lines, followed by each of the band members taking his turn as if they're in one of those B-side instrumental versions of an old James Brown record, the flip side of "Cold Sweat," for instance, James talking the band through the rhythm and hook, shouting "Give the drummer some," reconstructing the way the hit side was built until he laid his vocals over the music.

And so, not surprisingly, the novelty of making a national CD wears off by the second week. The places to go at night are limited, Aaron relates by phone one afternoon, so they tried a karaoke bar.

SIX PACKS TO GO it says on a large sign behind the bar. A cooler sits nearby, though instead of wading through the crowd that's listening to a woman singing a country song, they approach the bar to order. It doesn't matter. The song ends and another one doesn't begin. All of the karaoke enthusiasts turn to watch them. And when they ask the bartender for a couple of six packs he shakes his head. "We don't sell six packs," he says.

There's a moment when the band needs to decide whether or not to point out the sign and the cooler, whether or not to walk through the crowd and lift out a few six packs. They assess the looks they're receiving, the way their tattoos and haircuts and piercings are being evaluated by a roomful of strangers, and they decide to leave.

Two days later Aaron has another story to tell. He and Tony and Chris decide to leave town to scout the surrounding area. Fifteen minutes up the road they discover a strip club, what looks, after the karaoke bar, to be the hot spot, a place where differences are ignored because the focus is on alcohol and women's bodies. And all's well until things begin to wind down. Without the distraction of large breasts, the regulars start casting them the same looks as the karaoke crowd.

Worse, fueled by sex fantasies and hard liquor, the locals begin to articulate their skepticism about men who sport earrings and eyebrow piercings, men whose spiked hair glows unnaturally. It's not long before the taunts are a sort of karaoke of the eternal song of territorial defense, and it's time for Aaron, Tony, and Chris to call it a night.

So the evening is closing down, but when they head for the van, Chris, needing to leave behind one sign of defiance, jackhammers a fist down into the hood of a car he's passing, choosing, it turns out, a vehicle owned by one of the harassers, all of whom have followed them outside.

"Time to go," Aaron declares, hurrying to the van, and everything might have ended there, driving away to taunts and threats from people never to be seen again, except Chris unlocks his door, steps out and confronts them, taking the first shot and landing a punch to the face of harasser number one before the nature of the odds catches up with him.

Aaron and Tony, even if the best face is put on it, are ineffective. Chris is bloodied, and they do more to rescue him and cart him off than they do to wage war. When they arrive back at the studio, the word has spread by cell phone, and Nick is ready with the video camera to welcome the bloody hero home.

"It was another place for Hoover," Aaron says. "He knew all that karate stuff, and he wasn't afraid. That's all that fighting is—not being afraid and just wading in. I always think too much."

By December, when mixing has begun, the problems are more about music. "Everybody wants their parts to be heard," Aaron says. "Alex has to take control."

"That's why he's the producer," I try.

"Tony's the worst. He always wants the turntables amped up. Alex finally just told him off. 'You're just a DJ,' he said. 'You do your scratching and shut up.' But it's all good. I'll be home in time for Christmas."

And then there's an uncomfortable lull. The CD, at first announced as likely to be released in March, is delayed because it's discovered the name Driver was trademarked by another band just days before Universal sent in the paperwork. "We have to change again," Aaron says. "Now we're going to be Lifer. Nobody has that."

So it's April for the CD, and then, without explanation, May. Finally, the release date is set for August, the first single "Boring" ready to go for radio adds in mid July.

With so much time elapsing before the CD is released, the band is booked for a short tour with Saliva, Systematic, and Stereomud. If nothing else, the inactivity leaves Aaron at home on July 7, when his son Gavin is born, coincidentally, on my birthday.

Shannon and David drive in from New York. Derek rides with us to the hospital in Wilkes-Barre. Chris, when he arrives with a head-turning blonde woman, seems, at least for this afternoon, to represent the band.

After Betty Jo endures an hour with our family that melts into the beginning of an hour with hers, we take Aaron out for dinner. On the way to the restaurant "Boring" comes on the radio, the Wilkes-Barre rock station putting it in heavy rotation two weeks before it goes national. I hold the volume button down until it reaches construction-site decibel level. When it ends Aaron says, "That's the first time I've ever heard us on the radio."

I reach forward and turn it off. There's no point in hearing even one more song that afternoon. "So who was with Chris?" I say into the sudden silence.

Aaron laughs. "You won't believe this," he says. "That girl is Miss Nude Pennsylvania."

And for once our family has a unanimous reaction to something. Every person in the van hovers between "Really?" and "Wow!" until my wife says, "How do you meet somebody like that?" and everyone is relieved to laugh.

A week later, when Aaron and Betty Jo bring Gavin to Selinsgrove for the first time they joke about taking their son to a record store promotion. "His first rock show," Aaron says. "Drowning Pool played in the Gallery of Sound parking lot."

"I know," I say. "There's a picture of him on one of the fan sites."

Aaron stops smiling. "What the hell?" he says. "That's not cool."

"You're a public figure in Wilkes-Barre," I say.

"That doesn't matter. People need to chill out." He passes Gavin to me, privacy suddenly a matter of who is holding his son.

They start their first national tour in Nashville. "It was sold out," Aaron says. "It was nearly full even when we went on first."

They travel throughout the South, heading toward Florida just in time for the first hurricane of the season. I know about the bad weather before Aaron does because I watch the weather channel every day for the part of the country where the band is traveling, even when I have to watch it in motel rooms because we leave for vacation the following day, the Sunday before Lifer goes for adds with "Boring." We'll be able to hear the song all the way to South Dakota, I think, figuring a range of about two hours of listening around any big city , enough coverage that we should hear it half the time, or at least enough to know it's being played in Pittsburgh, Cleveland, Indianapolis, and Chicago, the cities stretching toward South Dakota like a connect-the-dots of marketing.

When we stop in Indiana on Monday we go into a record store where we see a list of CD release dates that runs through the end of August. Underneath August 17, along with twenty other names, is Lifer. "There you go," I say, and a teenage boy standing nearby asks us who we're looking forward to.

"Lifer," I say. "My son's the guitarist."

He grins. "That's so cool," he says.

But at the end of the day on Tuesday, we haven't heard a mention of Lifer on the radio. "Give it time," my wife says. "They're not superstars yet."

In Davenport, when I can't resist asking about Lifer in another record store, the clerk says they're not on the order list. "Really? It should be," I say, but it's a bad moment, one that brings an urgency to listening to every modern rock station within range of the van's radio.

The next day, in Cedar Rapids, the disc jockey spends thirty seconds hyping the next big thing, "fresh as just-baked bread for you," and I sit up, listening hard until he ends his introduction with "Puddle of Mudd."

"Well, there's the one new group that went into rotation this week," I say.

"There can be more than one," my wife says. "This song isn't that great. Maybe they're from around here or something."

By South Dakota, we've heard Puddle of Mudd a half dozen times, and listening to the radio from city to city is something I wished I'd never thought of. We walk the Badlands. We sit in the car among a herd of buffalo who eye us through the windshield. We spend a day driving between fields of corn, crossing Nebraska something like being on a boat out of sight of land, so few changes in the landscape I imagine us turning into one of those fields and disappearing as thoroughly as a failed solo ocean sailor.

In Cincinnati, the second week after the single's release, they're not on the published play list in the record store we browse. And when we pick up the Columbus station that Aaron had said was playing the song early, we hear, within ten minutes, Puddle of Mudd.

In August, just before the CD is scheduled to be released, Mark falls asleep driving to New Jersey on Route 80 after the band was rousted out early the morning after a Binghamton show for a record store promotion followed by a show the same night near the Jersey shore. Aaron tells me about this near accident immediately, how Chris, Tony, and Nick fell asleep within minutes of leaving Wilkes-Barre, how he tried to stay awake to keep Mark company but gave in when they reached New Jersey after Mark told him he was fine. "It couldn't have been five minutes," Aaron says, "and the bouncing woke me. We were in a field a hundred feet off the road, a mess of trees coming up, and there was Mark asleep at the wheel. I screamed at

Mark, and he woke up. Thank God he didn't panic and turn hard or we would have rolled, because that van with all that stuff behind it is really unstable."

I listen on the other end of the phone, at a loss for advice or even a phrase of fatherly relief. "How close to the trees were you?" I finally ask like a voyeuristic ghoul.

"Real close," Aaron says at once. "It was sort of a small side-of-a-hill grade where we were, and that probably kept us from going directly into them before anybody woke up. The other guys all acted like they thought it was funny later. It wasn't funny at all."

"You have to be in a real tour bus," I say, recovering my common sense.

"Either that or we're not going out," Aaron replies at once. "We already called Corey and demanded a bus. This has to stop."

"Good," I say.

"You know, Dad," Aaron says then, "I was the only one wearing a seatbelt. There's no telling how that would have worked if we'd gone into the trees."

In mid August Lifer packs so many people into a midnight madness sale they sell 1,200 CDs and get on the television news. The next night, even though I'm due to give a poetry workshop and a reading late the next morning in Washington, D.C., my wife and I drive to Scranton for the release show. Systematic and Stereomud, both high-energy bands that just toured with Lifer, open the show, revving up the crowd.

Breaking Benjamin fills out the lineup, playing, for this show, all originals. But by the time they're halfway through their set Tink's is a sea of murmurs and movement forward, the crowd, beers and cigarettes in hand, jostling for favorable sight lines. The place seethes, everybody roaring when the lights go down and then come up in rapidly flashing colors reminiscent of the garish shades of early color television.

By the time Aaron kicks into the opening riff of "Boring" everybody is fist pumping and throwing themselves into the music, most of the room singing along. I see Ben sitting on the side of the stage, and for a moment I think of the solid originals he just performed, how he might feel about all this attention going to a band that he once fronted, how nobody else in this crowd, most likely, is thinking of that part of the band's history right now. And then Systematic's guitarist comes on stage to join Aaron in a Deftones cover, the audience jacked up even higher by this visible acknowledgment of rock and roll coming-of-age.

Finally, the show closes in a familiar way with wholesale body-slamming when Nick roars the "Get the fuck up" call to chaos through-out "Heave." Standing with my wife and Betty Jo and Laura and Nick's girlfriend Beverly inside the crime scene tape Corey has used to set aside a space for "band family" to watch from, I'm convinced, for an hour, that Lifer can generate hundreds of CD-buying fans every time they perform.

We drive away, leaving Scranton at 2 A.M. I'm scheduled to be on stage 250 miles away at 11 A.M. Suddenly, the double shift I'd welcomed when the show began seems like a lousy idea. I drive until I feel like I'm going to kill us both, pulling onto the shoulder to let my wife take over. By now we're outside of Gettysburg, past 4 A.M. "Are you okay?" I ask, and Liz nods so unconvincingly that I can't fall asleep. Forty-five minutes later, near Frederick, Maryland, I ask her if she's okay, and she stays fixed on some middle distance, as if some-thing crawling on the hood of the van is what she wants to see more than anything on the highway. I ask again and her answer, audible this time, is a slurred "No." A minute later I'm back behind the wheel and determined to be asleep in a hotel bed before 6 A.M.

The clerk sends us to a room where the key card doesn't work. Not the familiar annoyance of trying to guess whether the card works better if shoved in more rapidly or more slowly, but the disaster of twenty repetitions, fast and then slower and then so slowly the card barely moves as both Liz and I use our unsteady hands.

Shortly after 6 A.M. security eventually comes to help us with what can only be described as a master card. "There you are," the security officer says, but when the door is open at last, it's obvious by the appear-ance of files and several boxes of Xeroxed hand-outs, that the reason we need security's assistance is because this is someone else's room.

Five seconds later I recognize its occupant—the man who has hired me to lead workshops, read my poems, and judge a poetry com-petition. He's registered all of the workshop leaders for rooms under his name, and whoever checked me in at 5:50 A.M. has apparently assigned me the first one that showed itself on his computer screen, ignoring the odd coincidence of one man living in seven different rooms.

By now at least three doors in the hall have opened, and none of them because the occupants are leaving for a 6:15 A.M. jog. I sit on the floor, my back against a wall. My weekend employer works the phones until someone appears with a new set of room keys. All's finally well at 6:30. My wife settles in to sleep until she wakes naturally, eats lunch, and spends the afternoon in the pool. I leave a wake-up call for 9:30, the latest I've slept in since college. I can't help but check the clock. It says 6:54. My ears are still ringing so loudly I imagine the phone sounding like a variation on the buzz and brrrrr that follows me into sleep, nothing that will wake me. And just before I fall asleep I remember Aaron telling me about their near-crash in New Jersey, the eyes and voice of my wife in Maryland. I think of myself driving home by myself from thirty shows at 3 A.M., ears ringing, trying to stay awake by listening to CDs turned up loud enough to scratch through the fuzz of tinnitus and exhaustion. Like Aaron and Liz, I always wear my seatbelt. If I crash, the paramedics won't have that to reprimand me for.

Despite the 1,200 CD head start from the midnight madness sale in Wilkes-Barre, Lifer sells around 2,500 CDs altogether the first week out, #50 on the Billboard Heatseekers chart, something designed to feature CDs by artists who have never had a release reach the regular Top 100. Not a disaster, but not promising; and the next week, when they sell 1,500 and there's still no radio play, it looks grim.

At least, to my relief, Lifer gets a tour bus, one sign of support from the label. In early September they're off to promote the CD before it is buried deep in the L section of record stores, those death-valley files where bands go when they're selling badly.

The tour has them playing a forty-five minute set before Dope, who have their own new CD to promote by opening for Cold, a band that's modestly charted, strong enough sales to guarantee getting to make another CD. Playing first in a three-band lineup means the crowds are usually small when Lifer walks on stage. Playing without radio support means those small crowds have little idea who Lifer is, and they have to sell their music in a hurry or suffer the impatience of hard drinkers who have queued up for Dope or Cold, all of it sponsored by Cutty Sark.

Touring will help promote the record, I convince myself daily. There are stories of word-of-mouth groundswells, bands that beat the odds of limited radio exposure, but I remember the tepid response to Boiler Room and the catcalls for Isle of Que, and less than two weeks into the tour Aaron doesn't sound like he's living the dream, even when some of the early dates are on the East Coast, where they have a following. "We mostly sell like twenty or thirty CDs at a show, something like that."

"Seed sold twenty tapes when you played in high school."

"Tell me about it. We do better playing on our own. It's not as cool as you might think."

Tuesdays and Thursdays are the mornings I write at home from 6 to 9 A.M., so I'm right out of the shower and eating my early lunch just before 10 when Derek calls. "Do you know what's going on?" he says in a tone that immediately makes me think "family disaster."

"What?" I try.

"Go downstairs and turn on the television," he says, and I'm momentarily relieved because I know this is national news, not private loss. And then I carry the phone down to the television and begin to watch, like hundreds of millions of others, the extraordinary aftermath of terrorism, the first tower falling before I can even manage "Huh?"

Every concern except for the safety of my children turns as petty as bickering over whose turn it is to take out the garbage. Within minutes, while Derek begins to try to reach Shannon, who teaches in lower Manhattan and doesn't have a cell phone, I'm on my way to the university because, inexplicably, I only have Aaron's cell phone number at work and Derek only has it at home. By fortunate chance, I think, Lifer is scheduled to play the night of September 11th in Philadelphia, the major city closest to us on the tour.

As if both of us trying simultaneously improves the odds, I call Shannon's apartment first. David is almost certain to be home, all of his actor-as-waiter hours scheduled around lunch or dinner. Between busy signals I walk down the hall to watch the news on a television somebody has wheeled into the department's common room. A plane crashes near Pittsburgh. Nobody in the room offers commentary, all of us transfixed and mute. I return to the office for a third try at reaching

New York City, this time starting to sort through the mass of Post-it notes on my desk, certain that one of them has Aaron's cellphone number. So when the phone rings as I'm searching I have it off the receiver and against my ear so quickly it thuds against my temple.
"This is fucked up, Dad," Aaron says at once.

"It's more than fucked up," I say.

"What the hell, Dad? What's wrong with people? We pulled off the road. We told the driver to stop, and we're sitting here waiting for Corey to call to tell us what's up."

"The show will be canceled."

"We told the driver to just turn around and start back while Corey gets his shit together, but here we sit."

"Tell him again. He works for you."

"Nick's in his face now. I think we're out of here. Shannon's close to this bullshit, isn't she? You talk to her?"

"Not yet. Derek's trying too."

"Talk to her. Call me back. You have the number there, right?"

"Right," I say, telling the truth, because halfway through the pile I've reached it. Aaron hangs up like a demand, and the phone begins to ring before I can dial the New York number again, Derek calling to tell me he got through to David.

"David has friends with cell phones who work near her school," he says. "They're checking for him." I nod as if he can hear it and give him Aaron's number, hanging up and immediately dialing it.

"Derek got through to David," I say as soon as Aaron picks up. "He's working on it. She would have been at school by then." And then I add, "It's probably a mile away," providing my daughter as much distance as possible from disaster.

"What's next?"

"I don't know."

"I was getting off this bus if it didn't turn around."

"It's turning, right?"

"Right. I gotta go. I love you guys."

Everything suddenly seems trivial. It's Mark's birthday. A Tuesday, it's when new CDs are released to record stores, whichever band going out today running up against the ultimate bad timing to release a dozen or so rock and roll tunes. It seems obscene to even think about entertainment. It seems obscene for my son to be performing for a living. I know this will be the most television I will have watched in one day since high school. My daughter, it turns out, spends the day making sure her students get connected to their parents. Many of them, if their morning class was on the south side of the building, have watched the second plane crash into the South Tower. The school, I learn later, is less than a mile away from the disaster site.

The tour, when it resumes the weekend after September 11th, doesn't improve Aaron's spirits. Sales are stagnant. And then, within weeks, Aaron tells me Mark has quit.

"It's a story you don't want to know," he says on the phone. "But we have to find a backup to tour with us. Definitely temporary, if you know what I mean, but what needs to be done needs to be done. We'll sort it out in November. Take our time then and do a real audition."

Aaron is calling from Missouri, the bus on its way back from Arizona because Lifer has a short break from the tour, long enough to rehearse the new bassist who has to finish the October and November dates.

"We hired some guy who's never going to work out," Aaron tells me from Wilkes-Barre two days later. "This is lame. You're coming to the show at the Crowbar, right? So you'll see when we come through State College. He's like Chucky Cleancut or something. He'll get fired the day the tour ends."

When I ask how sales are going, whether they're getting radio play anywhere, Aaron goes silent before he says, "If I want to know that, I'll have to call Corey. He stopped calling. It sucks."

A week later I invite three of my writing students to go to the State College show. When we get in the van there's no sense of going to a rock show. Aaron, who's riding with us because he wanted to take advantage of being nearby to spend one night in a real bed, is so subdued and somber we might be traveling to everybody's second try at the SATs.

Halfway to State College, as if he wants to prove how dismal things have gotten, Aaron calls Corey and asks about sales. "Sixteen thousand," he says to me after he hangs up. "Total." He shakes his head weakly. By doing the math, I know, without asking, that their sales have slipped to a thousand a week, maybe even below, not enough to support the expenses of keeping a band on tour.

Worse, for the first time I sense there's no camaraderie. We see Chris and Tony outside the club, but Aaron brushes by them with a "What's up?" and when we pass the new bassist, he doesn't introduce me, saying only "That's the new guy." The students drift off to get something to eat. Inside the club Nick is already busy cozying up to two girls in short leather skirts at the bar, nearly empty so early in the evening.

"They're the Cutty Sark girls," Aaron says. "They travel with the tour. They get paid to look like that. Nick's dreaming. You want to see the tour bus?"

"Of course," I say, and Aaron gives me the step-by-step tour, kitchen stuff and bunks, television and stereo. "Pretty cool, huh? This was Slipknot's bus before we got it."

Back outside, I shake hands with the driver, evaluating him as carefully as I do the pilots who walk through the gate at which I sit in an airport. This is the guy who needs to be reliable, who needs to stay awake all night like my father did when he worked alone in his bakery and slept all day. I don't want to see him with a beer in his hand.

On stage the new bassist, Roger, bounces around like he's in a pop-punk band like Sum 41. He's nearly frantic with energy, and yet he looks like he's in another band, all of his leaps and twitches the stock moves of a school boy in front of his bedroom stereo.

The rest of Lifer is as tight as ever, but the crowd is spotty with enthusiasm. There's only a small pit, hardly enough to put the bouncers on edge. Upstairs, there are a hundred people at the bar or sitting at tables, fueling up for something other than going crazy for Lifer. It feels as if I'm at a Strangers With Candy show before they arrived on MTV.

When Aaron walks upstairs before Dope's performance, there's barely a head turned. Nobody except maybe one of my students is going to buy me a beer in State College because I'm Aaron's father. In fact, nobody's looking as if they're sizing Aaron up. He could be anybody in this crowd, half of which have similar piercings.

Dope comes on looking like quintuplets, each of them with long, braided hair, each with no shirt. When they leap onto risers and point their guitars at the crowd, launching into a chorus of "Bang, bang, you're dead, fuckah," I think of Spinal Tap and fall into a funk as deep as Aaron's.

There's a pause between songs, the singer holding the microphone as if he has a public service announcement to make. Finally, he thunders, "This is for Osama bin Laden," and the crowd roars when the band repeats the rapid-fire chorus, "Die, Motherfucker, Die," the hosts of fists thrust into the air reminding me of those planned demonstrations against the United States in Middle Eastern countries.

"What's Mark doing these days?" I ask when Dope's set ends.

"He joined Breaking Benjamin," Aaron says matter-of-factly. "He's happier now."

Aaron's answer is so surprising I simply turn back toward the stage. When Cold begins their set with whiny songs that feature a singer who seems intent on standing perfectly still as a sign of angst, I round up my students for the seventy-five-minute drive home.

Fifteen miles into the trip I slide in the Lifer CD and play it from beginning to end. It takes us all the way to the school, ending with the acoustic version of "Perfect" just as we turn into the main parking lot. "They're so good," one student says, her tone calling up all the unspoken antecedents for pessimism.

The most upbeat phone call I get from Aaron is from Los Angeles three weeks later. They're playing the Roxy in a few hours. There are always industry people at L.A. shows, other bands who hang out afterward. "I saw Elton John in The Hustler Store an hour ago," Aaron says. "It was cool."

"As in *Hustler?*"

"Yeah. You know. Brand-name porn."

But when the band arrives home just before Thanksgiving, Aaron doesn't want to talk except to say, "We're home until January." And when I press him for what's in store for January, he simply says, "Waiting for February."

The good news is Lifer will be on the soundtrack CD for *The Scorpion King,* sure to be a best-seller with all the hype from *The Mummy Returns* and, because The Rock is starring, professional wrestling. "'Breathless,'" Aaron says, when I ask which song, and I tell him it's a good choice, that it's my favorite song from the CD, that it should be the next single, that releasing "Not Like You" as the second single, which is what Universal has just done to little radio response, was a bad idea, that maybe being on a soundtrack CD will successfully hype them.

"Settle down, Dad," Aaron says. "We're not going to get heard in the movie. It's one of those 'inspired by the movie' soundtracks. Godsmack is going to have the first single."

"It's still good to be included," I say, not ready to give up yet.

"It would have been way better if we'd gotten our ass in gear and had the new song that we recorded while we were on the road make it onto the CD."

So it turns out he's written a song specifically for the soundtrack, but by the time they recorded it, decisions had been made, none of which had anything to do with the quality of the song. "Here it is," he says, and Derek and I sit and listen when he slides it into the CD player in my basement.

The song thunders through the room. The guitar riff is so good I can't wait to hear the song played a second time. "It's excellent," I say at once, "maybe better than anything on the album."

"That's good to know," Aaron says, "because nobody is ever going to hear that song. Corey didn't push it. He thought Nick singing 'so alive' in the chorus was too much like the POD song that's been all over the radio."

"So it wasn't just timing?"

"That's what he says, but that's bullshit. We made it under the wire. He just didn't support it." He looks at both of us. "You want to hear something even worse?"

"Sure," Derek says, and I shrug, knowing we're going to hear it regardless.

"You know about *Not Another Teen Movie?* It's going to be like *Scream,* you know. It makes fun of all those high school flicks instead of goofing on horror movies. Well, listen up." And then he plays "Take On Me," a version so dreadful I barely recognize it's being played by Lifer.

"What's up with that?" Derek says. "It's all wrong."

"One more movie soundtrack missed," Aaron says. "Chris couldn't play it."

"What do you mean he couldn't play it? You did it on MTV. You've done it a hundred times live."

"I shit you not. He couldn't play it in the studio. He had to do take after take to even come up with this. A mental block or something."

"But what's up with Nick?" Derek asks. "Listen to this. It's lifeless. And that screaming. Who's that? Tony? Whose idea was that?"

"Not mine," Aaron says. "That's the only time I'm playing it," he adds, taking the CD from the changer and dropping it into a case, ending the discussion like a boy about to take his ball and go home.

When he visits for two days at Christmas there's still no sign of another tour all the way through the end of February, and Aaron starts right in: "You know what Corey says? 'It's the slow time of year.'"

And then, during the five-minute drive to the mall the day after Christmas, Breaking Benjamin comes on the radio, their demo of "Polyamorous" played on the university radio station as if it were riding up the modern rock charts. "Incredible," Aaron says. "It's not even a national release, and I hear they play this all the time, and yet they never touched any of our songs."

I don't know what to say, so I try, "It wouldn't have mattered if such a small station played Lifer. You would have sold maybe ten more records."

"That would be a spike for us."

He's so glum by late afternoon that I decide to drive to Luzerne to see the first Lifer show since the band came off the road in mid November. *Six weeks,* I think. The place will be packed, but even though Aaron seems pleased I'm going, I don't feel anything like joy or excitement.

My daughter and David, home for the Christmas week, hop in the car. It keeps conversation going, and I tell them, eventually, that I think Lifer is over, that playing one show in six weeks is a bad sign, that there's no "next tour," that they're not rehearsing or writing new songs, that "Not Like You" seemed such a bad choice for the second single that Universal must not be paying attention.

"And worse," I say, "anybody can see that Aaron is depressed about everything."

"I guess I'm going down with the ship," he'd said earlier, up to his knees in wrapping paper. When he'd given me a Lifer jacket as a present, I'd thought he'd been cleaning out his closet instead of pleasing me with one more rock and roll souvenir.

Inside the Voodoo Lounge, the front is roped off for the underage crowd, every available inch is stuffed with teenagers. I feel like I recognize half the crowd behind the rope, their leather outfits and old Strangers With Candy t-shirts so familiar that nothing turns my head except an old student from Susquehanna who arrives with hair arranged into massive green spikes.

Shannon and David find people to talk to. I lean against a railing, already bored with the Slipknot wannabees on stage, the singer growling and roaring, repeating "death" and "kill" so many times he's vocal graffiti. Aaron comes out, shaking hands with fans, but moving so quickly through the crowd he seems more like a campaigner than a guitarist. He picks up two beers at the bar, carries them toward me, and motions for me to sit at one of the small tables in the back.

"Listen to that," he says.

I nod, finish the beer I'd been holding, and take a sip of the one he offers. "It's packed," I say.

"Yeah. The same people that packed it last summer before the CD came out."

He seems distracted, like somebody waiting to punch in to work an assembly line night shift. He introduces me to the new bass player. "This is Ian," he says, and I remember he's told me he's the guy he can most easily talk to now.

"Gotta go to work," he says when he gets up.

The show is tight and professional. The mosh pit forms among the young, and behind the rope another small pit forms, more dangerous because it's so loose one or two drunks have an excuse to crash into fans who are just bouncing in place. A girl gets tripped. Another catches an elbow. The bouncers go to work.

Suddenly, without the rush of anticipation, the sense that this show is building toward something, all this thrashing and shoving looks as stupid to me as it would to my father.

The crowd screams for an encore, and when just Aaron and Nick come out they know it's the acoustic "Perfect" they're going to hear. The entire club goes quiet as Nick sings, not a hint of growl in his voice. It's plaintive and effective, and for the first time this night I'm paying attention without thinking of what's going on around the band.

Finally, the rest of the band reappears, and they launch into "Breathless," the song that's landed on the soon to be released *Scorpion King* soundtrack. It's rumored to be the third single, what will be the final shot for the band to get attention. Listening now, I'm certain it's my favorite Lifer song, Aaron spewing out the relentless riff, spontaneous pits forming. Even when Tony walks off stage, then Nick, and then Chris, Ian keeps laying down a bass track for that riff. Thirty seconds later, he's gone, too, Aaron still chugging until he lays his guitar down in a way that keeps a howl of feedback wailing from the suddenly dark stage, that electronic scream extending like the voice of someone plummeting from a cliff's edge.

And in that moment I am certain I've seen Aaron play with Lifer for the last time.

Breaking Benjamin

Less than a week after the show at the Voodoo Lounge, Aaron sits in for part of a set with Breaking Benjamin. A few days after that he drives to New Jersey and plays an entire show with them. "I learned thirty songs this week," he says on the phone. "I'm going to join if they want me."

I wait.

"I quit the band," he says then. "That's it. No going back."

"So you might not have any band to be in?"

"Better than waiting for those guys to wake up and admit Lifer's in the toilet."

"How pissed are they?"

"Real pissed. But they'll figure it out. They can get another guitar player. They're not doing any shows, so they have forever to get it in gear."

Despite his anxiety about looking like he's jumped ship, Aaron is excited for the first time since he called about Elton John in early November. He's convinced Ben's songs are better than Lifer's. Everybody in the band is cool with him joining. "I don't have to listen to so much shit," he says. "Freddie's putting the demo out there with record companies. He's playing the shit out of "Polyamorous," Dad. I can't even drive to the grocery store without hearing it. We could get signed."

"And if you don't?"

"You don't know what's going on, Dad. They've already show-cased in L.A. for Warner Brothers."

"But nothing came of it?"

"There's other labels out there."

In a movie script or a novel this would be such an obvious turning point it would seem like a feel-good formula—the second chance. And watching such a scenario, I wouldn't trust anything.

Living in it, I start to believe Aaron despite the fantasy-odds of being signed twice. The five-song demo is a knockout. Any one of the tunes could be a single on the radio. There are two guys in Breaking Benjamin who left a signed band. Selinsgrove has 6,000 residents, yet this would be the fourth signed band with a connection to the town. There are stories here, intrigue, the sort of conflict that makes a P.R. person beam.

And nearly at once the band is booked on a plane to Los Angeles. "We're showcasing for Rick Rubin," Aaron tells me. "You know who he is? He's huge."

"His name sounds familiar."

"Def Jam Records, Dad. He started it with Russell Simmons. The biggest name in Hip Hop. He produced Run DMC. The Beastie Boys." Aaron becomes animated. "The big Chili Peppers CD. The Black Crowes. He's huge."

The complication is that Ben refuses to fly. "He freaked out on the plane when they flew out for Warner Brothers," Aaron explains. "He started asking if the plane could land before Los Angeles. After 9/11, that didn't go over with the crew. He's going by train. He has to leave three days before the rest of us."

"And then get home three days after the rest of you?"

"Ask him some time, Dad. You don't know Ben. This isn't some temporary thing."

"Okay," I say, beginning to convince myself that something will come of this because the plane tickets have been paid for. But they return empty handed, nothing but disinterest from Rick Rubin who, apparently, can invest several thousand dollars in auditioning bands without worrying about what that investment might yield.

"He just listened and didn't say much of anything," Aaron says. "And then he was gone."

I hesitate, trying to conjure a supportive phrase. "Come to the next show, Dad. You need to check this out."

So in late January, only three months after I watched Lifer at the Crowbar, I go back there for my first Breaking Benjamin show that isn't followed by Strangers With Candy, Driver, or Lifer.

When my wife and Derek and I walk into the State College club, we have the place nearly to ourselves. Aside from about twenty friends of the band, there's no one on the lower level close to the stage, yet it's only half an hour until Breaking Benjamin goes on.

Upstairs there's another fifty people, all of them sitting at tables or at the bar. Nobody's claiming a spot at the balcony railings. I think of Rick Rubin's expensive indifference, what suddenly seem to be just rumors of other upcoming record label showcases, and Aaron's optimism about being signed for a second time.

The crowd triples by show time, though only a third of the two hundred people stand in front of the stage when Breaking Benjamin comes on unannounced, the most subdued beginning to a show I've seen since Strangers With Candy played in the cafeteria for my summer high school camp.

Derek and I go downstairs. Neither of us can watch sitting at a table as if Aaron were in a pop combo at the Holiday Inn. The small crowd by the stage sways so mildly in place I could hide among them, but I don't care. The new songs I'm hearing are excellent. If I haven't already learned the lesson of perception, this is a refresher course. The crowd upstairs, still growing, is getting revved for a band they know. Fifty minutes of unfamiliar original music is no way to seduce the house, but here I am being sold again, thinking *Of course they'll be signed,* wanting to turn around between songs and yell that foresight up the stairs. And then I muffle the apprehension that rears up like the ghost of Lifer by moving closer to the stage like a star-struck teenager.

Until just before the last song, Ben not only doesn't speak to the crowd, he also doesn't identify the band. "We're Breaking Benjamin," he says at last, his clipped and hurried speaking voice sounding disconnected from the passion of his singing. Afterwards, I stand near the stage with Aaron. The group of diehard fans crowd around Ben and Jeremy. "They're from the Grove," Aaron says.

And then one guy walks down from upstairs and yells, "You guys rock."

"Thanks," Aaron says.

"What was your name again?"

"Breaking Benjamin."

"Thanks, dude," he says. "I hope Stept On has you open for them again. Rock on."

"He's going to be disappointed," Aaron says. "This is the last time ever for this." He shakes his head as a stream of people come down the stairs to fill in the space around the stage. "This thing is taking off. For sure. Freddie's pushing us big time. He's giving us thirty spins a week."

"Can he get anything done more than hundred miles from Wilkes-Barre?" I say, trying to avoid telling him he's said this before.

"He's out there trying. He's really into us."

"What's in it for him?"

"He'll get points if we get signed. It'll all get worked out. He's way over the top sometimes, but what the hell, he's backing us and he gets heard, so it's all good."

I wait because it looks as if Aaron has more ammunition than Freddie's enthusiasm. "It looks like this guy Larry is taking us on as manager," he says then. "He's huge. He managed Kiss. He does Megadeth."

Optimism swirls around us like the chords of the first Stept On cover song in the room behind us. "We're showcasing again, Dad," Aaron says. "At Brew's Brothers in two weeks. There's at least eight labels coming."

I nod as if this arrangement is commonplace. At least eight labels? Aaron is so low-key he makes it sound as if Breaking Benjamin is showing up for a cattle call.

"It was cool," Aaron says, when I ask him about the show-case. "Some of it sucked."

Luckily, Derek went, as a guest of the band, to the pre-show din-ner provided by Atlantic Records at Brew's Brothers. "It was weird," Derek says. "It's not what you think. The band wasn't even paying attention to Atlantic. It was all Larry and Freddie. The band acted like they didn't care."

I think of spitball throwers in a middle school cafeteria, boys slouched in plastic chairs as a way of disguising the occasional flicks of their wrists.

"Atlantic was hesitating. The A&R guy started talking about pro-moting the demo EP for a while before making a full-length CD. That's when Freddie went balls out. He started going off on them. 'It's time to fuck,' he said. 'These guys will make Creed look like the Knack.'"

"Was Freddie wasted?"

"No. Not at all. He doesn't even drink. He was just being Freddie."

"Atlantic's out of the picture, Dad," Aaron finally says. "We don't need a label that wants to 'groom us.' Everybody was there—Universal, Electra, Columbia. Larry gave all the labels a number to shoot for. It was huge for an unknown band."

"Did Universal make an offer?"

"Yeah," Aaron says, "and it sucked as bad as the one Lifer got. They're out of the running, too."

"Didn't they remember you and Mark?"

"Yeah, but that didn't seem to be an issue. It's all about the money. And Hollywood was still standing at the end."

Aaron smiles. He has a punch line, after all.

In early March, at Club Xcess, déjà vu is putting on a per-formance—like the post-MTV buzz for Strangers With Candy, like the post-signing chaos for Lifer, this show, days after the official signing by Hollywood, is packed and seething with the conviction that Breaking Benjamin is the next big thing. Every song is suddenly important and memorable. Plus it's Ben's birthday, or at least within a day of it, so there's an excuse for shots to be passed up to the stage, Ben becoming unnaturally demonstrative between songs. Song requests are hurled from the crowd. Every chord and hook are approved of with whoops and screams. If I hadn't stood among a crowd like this at the Lifer shows in the weeks before the first single went to radio, I'd be ecstatic with superstar anticipation.

The crowd roars them back for two encores. The lights go up on enough happy faces to guarantee a successful midnight madness sale of the CD in Wilkes-Barre and Scranton, but then I see Tony standing to one side, the hood of his sweatshirt pulled up over his head as if he'd slipped inside to scout the enemy.

"Hey," I say, and he lights up, walking over to give me one of those urban secret handshakes I let him lead me through.

"We're getting new shit together," he says before I ask him about Lifer. "It's all good." And then two girls recognize him, and he tucks his hood forward, smiles, and leaves me with a "What's up?" in their direction.

"It's mostly cool with Lifer," Aaron says a minute later. "I talk to Chris now, but I hear Nick still has issues. If he thinks I betrayed him or something, he has it wrong. Lifer was over when I left."

When Ben and Mark pass, I shake their hands as a way of hold- ing off the fans that are swirling toward them. "Hollywood means California again," I say to Ben. "You going to fly next time?"

"Never," he says at once. "Not for anything. Mark knows."

"He got all pale and started squeezing my leg with his hand," Mark says. "He didn't let go until we were on the ground. It left a big sweat mark on my pants."

"A tour bus," Ben says. "A train. They're okay."

"What if you get huge?"

"Like Europe or something? A boat then. That's it."

Within a few weeks I hear that Tony has been fired by the rest of Lifer. "The band is going in a new direction," it says on Lifer's official web site. The fans, when I read the message board, are split on this one—half think Tony has been screwed and that the band is over, since three of the five members are gone; half buy the party line. "It's a better band now," somebody writes. "Fuck those quitters."

"Polyamorous" is going to be the first single, and Hollywood Records is willing to spend money on a video, a plan that attracts submissions of treatments from producers in April as the band, except for Ben, prepares to fly to Los Angeles.

"Ben's going by train," Aaron says. "He's already gone because it takes four days."

It looks as if the essential ingredient of rock video treatments is hyperbole. Every one of the five treatments Aaron gives me to read the night before he leaves says "thundering," "explosive," "intense," "extreme," and "incredible" as the adjectives for the performances of the band members. All of them claim "Polyamorous" is "kick-ass," "powerful," and, once again, "explosive." And five out of five guarantee the video will be "frenetic," "surreal," and, of course, "intense" and "explosive."

I try to imagine the band accepting the video proposal that puts them inside an enormous golf ball that's being pummeled by shots from a multi-layered driving range. Of course, the band's "powerful" performance makes them oblivious to the incoming barrage, but what a series of launched golf balls has to do with "Polyamorous," aside from the inevitable hot girls flirting with guys as they practice their strokes, is problematic. And though this treatment, as well as all the others, promises to exploit the title by showing lesbian fantasy, none of them even hint at two guys flirting.

But at least it's the only treatment that doesn't employ the word "gritty."

As in alley or in urban world or in deserted parking garage, where the video story ends with a car driving straight toward the band with no sign of "breaking." I have to fight off my skepticism about lousy-spelling script writers who inadvertently propose the tension created by a possible car explosion rather than the tension created by a car that will not stop. Not to worry, though, because this "surreal" scene ends with the car driving through the band that is "incredibly" untouched.

Aaron wants me to make a choice before he tells me which treatment has been accepted, and so I fly by the stock melodrama of a beautiful girl turning into an "OLD HAG!" and, though pausing, I put aside what I decide is my runner-up choice, the one that includes a cat fight sequence, that staple of male fantasy, in a "gritty" alley.

"This one," I say, pointing to the proposal to develop a video modeled after the movie *Sliver*. Lots of hidden cameras in a series of apartments. A full-time voyeuristic couple manipulating those cameras while they watch a multitude of screens. Beautiful young women being filmed in suggestive situations. Thankfully, Aaron confirms this is the one that's been chosen, the hyperbole restricted to sexual innuendo, which, after all, is what the song is all about. A girl's shirt is soaked and subsequently lifted over her head. A girl wrapped in a towel has just stepped from the shower. A girl reaches her arms over her head to stretch provocatively. Even more pointed, one girl slides her foot along the bare thigh of another.

It's the promise of pornography suggested but not delivered. Breaking Benjamin's song will substitute for the orgasm-producing sex. For three minutes, at least. Aaron points to the director's name. "Gregory Dark is huge," he says. "He's done videos for Linkin Park and Britney Spears. He's done Staind and Counting Crows."

I think of the video Universal made for "Boring," how cheaply it was produced, the band replaying the song thirty-one times (Aaron counted) in front of a group of fans who obliged by going nuts for two hours, hoping they might be spliced into scenes of the band performing. How that video was shown only on MTVX, an outlet for rock videos that no longer exists. How none of the band members even received his own copy as a souvenir. Aaron has never mentioned the director's name.

Aaron gathers up the set of faxed treatments. "It's going to be a while until I see you again," he says, "so here's the Lifer story you've been wanting to hear." *Which one is that?* I think, but I put my feet up on the couch and settle because I can tell this isn't a one-minute anecdote.

"It started out to be the best day on the whole tour. We had the day off in Arizona, so we rented a van, and the bus driver drove us all way out into the desert to some lake where we rented a boat and jet skis. It was a great time. Everybody was giving the jet skis a go and having a few beers. It didn't seem like a big deal when the boat stalled after we decided to head back in, but it all went downhill from there."

Aaron studies me for a few seconds before he goes on. "Nobody came out to tow us. Nobody even answered the phone, and guys were getting pissed. We were out there with nothing to do but drink and bitch until some big houseboat came by and towed us."

"Houseboat?" I say, picturing a floating slum.

"Not that kind of houseboat," Aaron says. "It was a rich guy's houseboat, almost like a yacht, and full of all these businessmen having a party, free drinks for all of us all the way to shore, and then, of course, Nick went into the bar on shore to keep at it, and we followed him and stayed until everybody was stupid. And then when our driver was ready to take us back and everybody was in the van, Mark started screwing around. You know, poking me and punching me, stupid shit, halfway to pissing me off, so we started wrestling around and next thing you know punches are thrown and we're outside the van and Mark loses it and everybody else goes after him because we all know he's going to quit."

Aaron pauses, and I sit up in spite of myself. "Mark was crazy," he says, "and then everybody was crazy. Nick started saying all this stupid shit like "I hope you and your girlfriend rot in hell," and then Mark went off on him, and we're trying to hold him back. Meanwhile, all of a sudden Nick climbs up on the top of the van roof with a big rock ready to heave it down on Mark. He looked like a skinny Conan the Barbarian up there. You know, the whole pose with the big-ass rock over his head. It was real scary by then. It was more about Mark quitting than anything else. Guys were really pissed."

I lean forward and have to ask, "So where's the van driver through all this? How does something like this stop? You're in the middle of nowhere, and Mark has to ride with you."

"The driver was the driver. He drove away when we told him to.

He'd had about enough by then, so we left Mark out there."

"In the desert?"

"Forty miles from where we were staying. He had to hitchhike. And he'd lost a shoe in the scuffle, so he had that to deal with."

I leave the question about how you move on from an incident like this unspoken, but Aaron knows what I need to hear. "He played with us the next day. It was our biggest show, a festival with Staind and Alien Ant Farm and Lit and Jimmy Eat World. We were playing in front of 15,000 people all at once, and then that was it. We threw all his stuff in a garbage bag and tossed it out of the bus."

"How did he get home?"

"We gave in. He picked up his stuff, and we let him back on, and we rode all the way to Pennsylvania, and that was the last of that. That's not what made him quit. I didn't even blame him. I was already thinking about quitting. I wanted the band to get better, and those guys just wanted to live the life."

Aaron slouches back down in his chair, and I put my feet back up, both of us quiet until he says, "You want to know this stuff, right?"

"Yes," I say. "I do."

"I was one unhappy dude the rest of the tour. The new guy sucked, the band was going nowhere, and the other guys kept acting like everything was cool. The new guy thought he had to bounce around to be hip or something, but he was all the time missing notes until I told him to stand still and get it right. At least he listened, but I was sick to death of playing "My Room" every night to the early shift. We played it first for every show. Every night. No matter what I said."

"You couldn't just walk away. Mark left when you had a week off."

"Joe Perry," Aaron says. "You know who Joe Perry is, don't you? Aerosmith? He threw his guitar down in the middle of a show and walked off stage. I thought about it, throwing my guitar down and quitting right there in the middle of a show, but I toughed it out. Nobody else seemed to get it. We were down to selling two hundred CDs a week by the end of the year. I knew we were going to get dropped. We didn't get dropped because I quit."

Second Time Around

"Check this out." Aaron says, slipping a cassette into my VCR. It's Memorial Day, and he's just back from Los Angeles where Breaking Benjamin has finished six weeks of recording the CD that has been named *Saturate*. And when the familiar intro to "Polyamorous," the song that will soon be shopped to radio, washes over the first image of a man focused on a bank of monitors, I know I'm about to see how their first music video has been transformed from the hyperventilating prose of a treatment to videotape.

I'm hooked at once: the band playing in an empty swimming pool, that couple outlined on the page watching closed circuit television screens that simultaneously show the scenes laced with sexual innuendo taken by hidden cameras—sex play in a kitchen, a woman in a bathroom fresh from a shower, two women toying with each other while an oblivious man sits between them. The scenes seem instantaneously familiar yet fresh. Each band member gets to play in a scene—Mark strums his bass while the kitchen woman stretches with desire; Jeremy drums as the women look hungrily at each other; Aaron steps from the shower stall playing his guitar, the towel-clad woman within arm's reach.

In fact, it's so mesmerizing I wish the song was twice as long, that another chorus or two would let the sex scenes play out. The camera is so intent on the women's bodies that the song seems to explode each time the band reappears in the empty pool. I start thinking in the hyperbole of the treatment and know that Gregory Dark, director of pornography as well as music videos with Britney Spears, Linkin

121

Park, Counting Crows, and Staind, has delivered on the promises of his treatment. Watching the video a second time, I think of teenage boys wanting to see this video again and again, each time associating the song with sexual fantasy.

"It's first-rate," I say.

"Yeah, it is," Aaron says. "The only downside is all the people in Wilkes-Barre who think I'm the asshole who ruined Lifer by quitting."

And then I think of my daughter who, while visiting Los Angeles in April, took pictures of Aaron standing in front of a billboard promoting the soundtrack for *The Scorpion King*, the big-budget movie starring a professional wrestling hero. Over Aaron's left shoulder in all of the shots is a list of rock bands, including Lifer, that have songs on the CD. Four months after he and Mark left the band, that billboard seems eerie with memory, the two of them, even though Lifer is in danger of being dropped by their label, cranking out the song "Breathless" on CD players in over half a million homes and cars by now.

Five weeks later, the first time I sit among all four members of Breaking Benjamin at the same time, we're at a party eating cake and ice cream. It happens to be my birthday, but they're not humoring me by celebrating like grade-schoolers. Aaron's son Gavin is one year old today, turning my own anniversary into an afterthought.

Laura, now married to Mark, is pregnant. The due date is September 11, which is his birthday and the anniversary of catastrophe. It's a slew of coincidences, this table so full of unlikely events that the extraordinary fortune of Aaron and Mark being signed and releasing CDs from two major record labels in just over a year seems almost commonplace.

Right now Breaking Benjamin is on the cover of *The Album Network*, the trade magazine for music radio. The magazine lies in the middle of the table so anyone could glance from publicity picture to band member, comparing image to real life. A shaved head, an arm-length tattoo, a menacing expression—that's Mark in the photograph; but in context, sitting beside his pregnant wife, Laura, those highlights fade into the conventional gestures of family-man-to-be. Nose rings, tongue piercings, multiple earrings—every member of the band is decked out in the stuff that inspires head-shaking in the older relatives at the next table. But, after nearly three years of following aggressive rock, I have to concentrate to even note their sizes and shapes.

Aaron holds his son on his lap, letting Gavin gorge on ice cream. By the end of the afternoon, unused to hours of junk food, Gavin will be sick, but for now he's relishing a smorgasbord as exotic as truffles and squab to a one-year-old.

Last week Breaking Benjamin had the second most added single in "active rock." Fifty-three major-market stations are suddenly playing "Polyamorous," exactly what the band needs to generate attention for the end-of-August release of the CD. More stations are adding it this week in July, so there's something to celebrate besides birthdays. Jeremy's girlfriend, Yvette, turns to a list of smaller stations that have added Breaking Benjamin—St. George, Waterloo, Sault Ste. Marie; nobody in the band recognizes the location of these cities, but when she reads the names they sound like New York, Los Angeles, and Chicago.

"Under the Radar," the heading reads at the top of the page, but every spin on every station adds a blip on the screen. What's more, there is only one feature article in the entire magazine, and it's a two-page spread on Breaking Benjamin, enough to help all of us swallow and enjoy as much sugar and grease as Gavin.

Ben and his girlfriend, Candace, present me with a birthday card that features a dog that looks as glassy-eyed as a fan who has been drinking hard through three warm-up bands. "Sorry about the dog," Ben says. "It looked funny when we bought it."

"It's still funny," I say. "If I eat any more birthday cake, I'll look just like that."

"See?" Candace says, and he looks like he's been let off with a warning for speeding. "You should be glad he's not asking you what's up with this vampire look you have in every picture."

"That's because he never goes out of the house in the daytime," Aaron says, and stories of Ben's addiction to video games get tossed around the table—consecutive hours of playing that reach double figures, the multiple formats he owns—PlayStation, X-Box, a half dozen others so obsolete they're infused with nostalgia.

"I went outside every day for a week trying to get tan for the photo shoot," Ben finally says.

"With the right makeup, you could star in *The Crow 2*," I say, and Ben perks up.

"I love *The Crow*. It's the second-best movie ever made," he says, and then he looks embarrassed again. "I can't say that in front of a professor."

"What's the best?" I say.

"*Edward Scissorhands*." Ben watches my expression as if he expects me to cringe.

"It's okay," I say. "We're not in class."

And right then, an hour into spending time with Breaking Benjamin, I understand this band won't create a book's worth of crazy stories, that I have students in my college classes who have more adventurous lifestyles. Every one of them has a wife or a steady girlfriend; one has a baby and another will have one soon. They're delaying the first tour so Mark can spend time with the new baby when it arrives. Aaron is remodeling the house he's bought. If the *Behind the Music* crew showed up to interview and film, they'd apologize for coming to the wrong address. But I also know, rereading the familiar locations of the stations playing their song—Philadelphia, St. Louis, Detroit, Milwaukee—that regardless of what happens from here on out, Breaking Benjamin will be significantly more successful than Lifer.

And then finally, after hours of pop oldies have bleated from the speakers set up on the back porch, Aaron slides in an advance, unmixed copy of Breaking Benjamin's CD. As soon as Ben's first recorded scream roars across the yard, a crunch of guitars chasing after it, the older relatives at the other table shift in their chairs, sitting up.

"This is the music they do," one of Gavin's great-aunts says.

"Heavens," another says.

They look knowingly at the band. "The kids like it," the first one says.

And so do I.

"There's a new video," Aaron says on the phone a few days later.

"Why?" I say. "The first one was wonderful."

"Hollywood hooked us up with a new video game for PlayStation 2. Four of our songs are on the game."

"So what's different?" I ask.

"The story is gone."

"So all the sex footage is washed out?"

"Yep. We're still there, though. The game's called *Run Like Hell.*"

I start to imagine blazing guns and bloody victims, twelve-year-olds screaming "Die, motherfucker!" as they waggle a joystick. I think of a quarter million dollars, the cost of the original video, fluttering away in a thunderstorm of tens and twenties.

"It's not what you think," Aaron says. "Wait till you see the animation. And anyway, it's science fiction."

I go to the web site for a preview. The video game has animated space travelers and alien monsters. The woman, abducted by the aliens, has the impossible figure of boys' fantasies. The man is stoic and determined and fearless. The preview is stuffed with promise of weapons and battles and carnage.

And when Aaron visits a week later, sliding the new video into the VCR, the action figures look as familiar as R2-D2 and C3PO. Thankfully, the band's sequences in the empty swimming pool remain, and the song doesn't have overdubs of screams and crashes, but there's an inevitable story line that makes me think the phrase "selling out" as I watch. That stoic hero accelerates into rescue mode. Explosions follow while the music drives to a climax, and when what looks to be a space station turns into a roiling cloud of flaming gas, the scene coincides with Ben's last, definitive shout.

Anyone but a video fanatic or a marketing expert would agree that this version isn't as interesting as the original, but I see a hundred thousand boys playing this game, Breaking Benjamin roaring through their speakers, and when Aaron tells me that the newest game in this genre has sold a million units in Japan even before it went on sale in the United States, I know the meaning of "naïve in business."

I think of Ben playing the game, rapt with chasing down monsters borrowed from the *Alien* special-effects department. When I show Aaron the *Run Like Hell* website, I notice that a dozen new Breaking Benjamin hits pop up on *Yahoo!,* all of them featuring promotions for *Run Like Hell* and PlayStation.

Two weeks later I drive to Wilkes-Barre and the Staircase Club for the first of a flurry of final shows before the CD is released and the band goes on the road to promote it. If I was worried about how things were going locally, I can stop now, because even though it's nearly three hours until Breaking Benjamin performs, the large lot is filled, the field next to it is filled, and the shoulder of the four lane highway is clogging with cars parked foolishly close to late-night weekend drivers.

I park in the lot of a store a quarter mile down the road and walk back, passing two cars simultaneously parking in a field that obviously doesn't drain well, mud spattering up as they skid into a low spot. "Fuck!" one driver says as he gets out, but he's complaining about stepping into mud, not about how deep his car has settled.

"We'll need a tow to get the fuck out of here," the driver of the other car says, and they both laugh, slogging up to the shoulder.

"You'll see mullets," Derek had said five months before, preparing me for my first Breaking Benjamin headliner show the week after they were signed. "It's not like Lifer," he'd said then. "You don't have to have multiple piercings and visible tattoos to get in."

He was right. The two guys in front of me in the line that night wore NASCAR hats and twin shoulder-length mullets that would qualify them for consideration for the annual mullet calendar my sons exchange at Christmas as joke gifts. I saw it as a good thing that Breaking Benjamin reached into rural Pennsylvania, though when I noticed guys wearing jackets emblazoned with fraternity letters I felt as if I'd wandered into a late-night party at the university where I teach.

Back then I'd seen Breaking Benjamin only three times with Aaron in the band, and always as an opening act. That night it had been a preppy guy and his girlfriend who'd discovered I was Aaron's dad, they and two other college students clearing maybe six inches of room around me, giving me the equivalent of penthouse space for the rest of the show.

So now, after I get inside, I'm almost relieved when everybody on the side of the room where I wait for Aaron looks like a refugee from a Lifer show. Halter tops, leather, tank tops that bare tattoos, chains, spiked hair—it's all reassuring.

The most distinctive tattoo, because it is unmistakably home-made, so badly drawn it makes me think of stain remover and sandpaper, bleach and skin grafts, features dice on a guy's shoulder. The sides with three dots face out, the sides with one dot and two are just visible from the land of lousy perspective. "Stop staring," Aaron says, suddenly standing beside me. "He thinks it's great or he wouldn't be wearing a wifebeater to show it off."

I shrug, but I can't pull my eyes away before I evaluate the tattoo just below the dice, a circle of elephants linked trunk to tail around his bicep. "The elephants look professional," I say.

Aaron nudges me to turn away. "Yeah, but he stole that from Flea," Aaron informs me. "It's not that cool."

"So there's a Chili Peppers tattoo set?"

"It looks that way."

I take one more glance at the dice, how the frayed, raggedy wifebeater practically spotlights the guy's shoulders, and then he notices Aaron, smiles, and steps toward us, hand outstretched. "You guys fucking rock," he says.

Over his shoulder I see a guy who could win a System of a Down front man look-alike contest. He has the entire Serj Tankian look, sculpted beard and all. Two years after Strangers With Candy shows were flooded by Fred Durst look-alikes, created without much trouble by reversed red caps and a mannered slouch, this fan has gone the distance, working on that beard, I imagine, since he first watched the video for "Chop Suey" nearly a year ago.

"Props to you all," the dice-man says, and when he walks away Aaron says, "You'll like this. Hollywood made us go to New York for Media Training this week."

"Media training?" I think of men in business suits, consultants with flip charts or power-point presentations.

"The label thinks we screwed up our first interviews."

I remember the extended one from *The Album Network,* but everything comes back as harmless. "You know," he says, "Ben running down other bands. Ben talking about his songs as if what he's doing is ripping off riffs."

"Mark and Jeremy hardly even talk."

"But we all had to suffer together. They brought in this Ur-Nazi. She read to us from our interviews and made them sound like shit."

"Did the lessons take?"

"For now. She monitored the ones we just did. But Ben is pissed."

I follow Aaron into the dressing room as a warm-up band finishes its set. We're no sooner inside than their drummer is carried in, his arms draped over the shoulders of the singer and the bassist. "Oh shit," he says. "This sucks."

"His leg is fucked up," the singer explains, letting the drummer slide down into a chair. An ice bag is tied to the drummer's calf, so securely in place I know it's been there throughout their forty minute set. His hair is dyed so white that when he moves he's a human strobe light, but he props the ice-bagged leg up on a second chair and lets out one long moan before he smiles.

"I'm scheduled for surgery next week," he says. "It's fucked that I can't play for a while."

Explanations get passed around the room like beer. The most convincing is he has repetitive stress syndrome, that he plays the drums for hours, even on the days the band has a show. For weeks now his calf has locked up into something like a cramp nearly every day, but he's toughed it out for tonight.

"I wanted to make this gig," he says. "Breaking Benjamin fucking rules. They'd have to amputate to keep me off the stage."

"Fuck yes," a guy in an orange jumpsuit says. I recognize him as the front man for Cyphilis, one of the bands that regularly opens for Breaking Benjamin. His head is shaved except for a spiked Mohawk. On stage he's an hour of rage and obscenity, but here, close up, his smile is so benign that his performance sneer seems as artificial as a Nixon mask.

Back on the floor, when the last warm-up band comes on, Aaron tells me the drummer sports a Breaking Benjamin tattoo. "Really?" I say. "The BB logo like you guys all have?"

"No," Aaron says. "Us. Our faces."

"Like Mt. Rushmore," I say, and Aaron laughs, but I evaluate the drummer, who looks like an otherwise sane person. Suddenly the fact that he's wearing a T-shirt that features the cover of *Saturate,* the not yet released CD, seems a sign of lunacy. The blood cell design appears to be pulsing, the Breaking Benjamin logo of interlocked Bs inside of it a red-hot brand. Somewhere on that drummer's body is an inked recreation of my son's face. I think of the poorly drawn dice I saw earlier. I imagine my son's face drawn fat or thin because of proportions miscalculated. Washington. Lincoln. Roosevelt. Jefferson. Those presidential faces turn into fun-house caricatures.

Ten minutes later Aaron gets a wave from the door of the dressing room. "You're on your own," Aaron says to me. "Have fun."

I automatically move forward, find a place in front of the sound board where I can make sure I'm not surrounded. As soon as the last warm-up band walks offstage, a woman in front of me who looks to be sixteen but holds a beer in one hand picks at her black halter top with her free hand.

"I'm going to give Ben a major boob flash," she says to her two companions, both of them as young-looking as she is.

"Boob flash? I'd like to go right down on him," one says. All three seem to peer my way as if I'm a spy from the country of fathers, but none of them appear embarrassed. They're looking at a fourth young woman bringing four beers. KIMM, it says across the back of her shirt as she skids past me and hands out the Sam Adams Light the club is selling at a promotional discount.

"You see Aaron?" she shouts. "He just walked by you guys. He's just the cutest thing ever put on this earth."

"The Fink lover," the boob-flash girl says. "Tell him that to his face and hope for the best."

I see Chris walk by, and when I say "Hello," he pauses to talk. "We're trying to get signed again," he says. "There's interest. You know. Showcases we can do. We have a shitload of new stuff."

"Good," I say. "I'm glad."

"Yeah," he says.

I nod, but then neither of us have anything to add, and Chris wanders toward the stage door as if he's just remembered he's scheduled to perform. Suddenly, Butch and Hyland and a half dozen other regulars from fifty Strangers With Candy/Lifer shows pause beside me as they shove forward. Butch hands me a beer and smiles. "Back in the game," he says. Tonight, he has a stylized snake of thick hair zigzagging from his forehead to the base of his otherwise shaved skull. Two of the guys are wearing Strangers With Candy shirts. I half expect Lifer to come on stage when Freddie, the DJ who's pushed Breaking Benjamin for six months, fast-talks his way to the end of his introduction, and the crowd, including Butch and Hyland and all the rest of the old-timers, as if it shares that thought, suddenly surges forward and packs together, fists raised, leaving a full stride's worth of space in front of me as Breaking Benjamin opens with "Phase."

Immediately, I feel at home, reassured when the crowd sings along, when hundred of arms extend in the ubiquitous index and little finger sign of approval, when a pit forms and bodies begin to crash together. The biggest difference is the show seems more professional, if only because the band has props now, large Breaking Benjamin logo flags, and the light show includes images reminiscent of an old Jefferson Airplane show. Even Ben's patter between songs is smooth, smatterings of encouragement to the crowd and thank-yous instead of the old routine of "Let's get fucking crazy" and "Is everybody drunk yet?" Media Training be damned, yet it's working.

And above all, they're being filmed by a young woman who is not a fan. She moves among the band, stands inches from Ben as he sings, focuses on Aaron's guitar, then his face, then turns toward the crowd. The record company, I'm sure, has paid her to record this show. I think of Aaron telling me the company executives are flying in to watch. I think of the two videos, the commercial tie-ins, the MP3s and ads on websites. It's not at all like Lifer, when there were thousands of messages on fan sites but few hits that took me to radio station sites, play lists, and on-line reviews. Breaking Benjamin, at least so far, isn't struggling without radio play and advertising. The upcoming first tour, though modest, has Miller Lite as a sponsor and Breaking Benjamin as the headliner.

And then the crowd separates, and I see a girl doubled over, her face pale as she struggles to take a breath. I'm sure she's taken an elbow or a fist in the stomach. I think of the inhaler in my pocket, wonder whether she's asthmatic and careless. But then another girl is guided through that makeshift gate, sweat-soaked and moaning, her nose bloody. And then a third who holds the side of her head where I'm certain she took a flying elbow because the pit, three songs into the show, has gotten past the bouncers and torn into the part of the crowd that is happy to simply bounce and sing along, the part that is 80 percent young women.

I watch as a huge guy with an enormous mullet slides into the turmoil. The nearby soundman, as if on signal, shines a thin beam of light into the chaos, and the combination of the threatening man and the light calms the breakaway pit into a stop-action scene.

Plainclothes bouncer, I think, smiling to myself, taking note of his shirt, the intricately connected demons stretched across his back looking like a symbol for a private room in hell. He has mystery on his side. Even the sweat-soaked drunks have a sense that he might be the dark angel of mayhem. Nobody questions his not wearing one of the bright yellow STAFF shirts.

So for two songs at least, the mosh victims emerge from deep in the pit—two guys comparing cuts across their cheeks, a real bouncer leading a man with serious bleeding from his scalp. "He took a bottle to the head," the bouncer says to the soundman, and I remember Sam Adams Light, the upscale brand had become a weapon. When I push forward I notice a collection of two dozen guys who have the long-term felon look—shaved heads, no necks, shoulders and arms built up from years of weightlifting. They crash into each other during "Next to Nothing," the token mellow song that all the women stand still for, singing along.

And then I retreat, and the crowd closes up again, the band beginning "Polyamorous," so often played on the radio by now that everybody is transfixed and euphoric. It's better than twenty bouncers at controlling the crowd.

Afterwards, I stand in the dressing room. "Another Fincke," Ben says, when he sees me. "Now I have to watch what I say."

He tells the nearest fans to check us out. "The Finckes," he says, "you see that look they have? They're too smart."

"Heredity," I offer.

"That's it," Ben says. "You can tell they're always thinking. And you should see the littlest Fincke. The three Finckes—they're like the wise men."

The fans glance at me oddly, and I hear them considering my age. They know about Aaron's son, Gavin. They know Aaron is twenty-five. Addition is working the room. Totals are being assessed.

I feel like a middle-aged man, wrung out and dehydrated, my arthritic knees aching, my back sore. I've lived through three years of close-up rock and roll, and here, less than a month from record release and a year of tours, it's punctuated with bottled water and hand-shakes, with Ben somehow thinking, when I joke that he should call me Doctor Fincke instead of the formal and childish Mister Fincke he habitually says, that I have an MD.

"Doctor Fincke," he says. "I never knew that you did that too."

I try to decide among "giddy in the moment," "vodka in the water bottle," and "he really believes that." "It's not what you think," I say, and then I hurry to add, "But it's close enough" before he's surround-ed by young women dressed in the cleavage-makers and thigh-reveal-ers of rock and roll cheerleaders.

The following day Derek drives the forty miles from where he lives to have dinner with us. We gorge on chicken wings, but all of us, for this night, drink water or soda, and so when we walk outside it seems natural to hike to the soft ice cream shop five blocks away.

Chocolate. Whipped cream. Maraschino cherries. We do the whole elementary school routine, all of us busy with slurping and lick-ing when Jeremy walks up from a side street with Yvette.

It's one of those scenes you can't put into a short story because it sounds so sentimentally contrived—half of a major label rock and roll band eating ice cream together by accident in a small town in the mid-dle of Pennsylvania. And there's more. Derek graduated from high school with Yvette; my daughter went to high school with Jeremy. And what's more, as we talk in the twilight, Jeremy tells us his father is right at this moment performing for the "open mike" in the bar on the next block, playing a guitar and singing.

When we all look around we notice the Moose across the street, where Jeremy performed with a local band playing covers for lodge members one or two generations older. Which brings us to joking about how that early version of Breaking Benjamin won the Battle of the Bands at Susquehanna University, how Ben, Aaron, Chris, and Hoover had gotten to open for Cypress Hill in front of more than a thousand people.

In Central Pennsylvania, four years before, Cypress Hill fans were white boys wearing pants sagging to crotch level, underwear on display, and oversized sports-logo shirts. Derek, Liz, and I had free tickets, and we watched those boys shuffle down the aisles, unable to walk naturally because their pants dragged on the ground. Some of them had girlfriends, and if they did, they walked with one hand under the back of the waistband of their pants. Urban hand-holding, I said to myself, and then I looked around, hoping to see at least a small group of rural teenagers who were there to crowd the stage and scream for a band that had never played to more than a hundred people at one time.

There's a video of that performance, maybe a hundred and fifty fans standing close while nearly a thousand others slump in their seats throughout the auditorium. Except for Hoover, who sports a pocket watch chain and an urban-look knit cap, the band is dressed as if they're going to work at the ice cream stand where we're reminiscing. Nothing about them except the music suggests a career in rock and roll.

And even now, the Billboard charts—"Polyamorous" is #26 on Mainstream Rock this week and rising—seem unconnected to any of this. The young skater boys who crowd into the ice cream line are more boisterous and theatrical than either Aaron or Jeremy. By the end of this month *Saturate* will be one of the CDs those boys will lift and examine at the record store in the mall, either dropping it back in its slot or carrying it to the counter. They'll have forgotten they've brushed against half of the band they're blaring from CD players and pronouncing "awesome."

And for sure they won't know that for the past three days a hypnotist hired by the record label has been working to cure Ben of his fear of flying. That Ben spent four days each way going to Los Angeles to record because he chose to ride a train instead of joining the band on a plane. That when Aaron did an interview this week with a British promoter who asked, "When is this great band coming over to let us see them?" all Aaron could do was say, "We'll see" because nobody can imagine Ben sailing to England, even if it's to promote, as an early reviewer has said, a CD that is "one insane scream followed by nonstop good music."

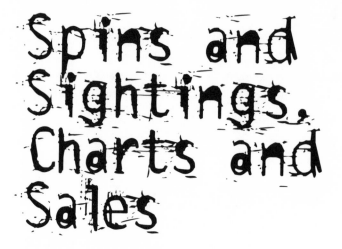

Spins and Sightings, Charts and Sales

"All the good stories are about Strangers With Candy and Lifer," Aaron tells me. "We're a band, not a soap opera."

When I tell that to Derek on the way to the record release show, he agrees. "That means boring," he says. "These guys could be working in an office."

We've just walked out of the Williamsport Circuit City, ninety minutes from Wilkes-Barre, and the CD is sold out, a good sign. Derek is right; if the band walked through that Circuit City one by one, they wouldn't turn anyone's head. "It's cool that it's just their music," Derek says, and I give him an honest nod.

The Voodoo Lounge is hosting the record-release show, and the venue is way too small to accommodate the crowd. As soon as we push our way to the bar and then into a space near the soundboard I remember the terrible ventilation this place has, the times I've had to go outside for fifteen minutes out of each hour for an oxygen break. Instinctively, as if I were a New York City tourist feeling for his wallet, I check my pocket for my inhaler.

It's a place, though, that's supported Breaking Benjamin as they evolved from the opening band for Strangers With Candy and Lifer into a headliner both without and with Aaron on guitar. So it's odd watching the band here because it's the site of Aaron's last show with Lifer, yet now, eight months later, he's taking the stage with another band that's been signed, been recorded, and been released since that depressing post-Christmas show.

And lately I've heard enough, and so has he, to combine exhilaration with optimism because "Polyamorous," this week, is at #21 on Billboard's Mainstream Rock chart, its spins still increasing, which means there's a reasonable chance for the CD to chart next week rather than have its sales confined to within an hour's drive from Wilkes-Barre and Scranton. "Polyamorous" is being played on a hundred large-market radio stations; somebody who lives more than a two-hour drive from here will buy this record.

So this time around I don't measure the success of the band by the intensity and size of the mosh pit. I don't turn to see if the crowd is at crush-size all the way to the rear exit. And I don't count the bouncers vs. drunks for incidents. I give myself up to knowing that the band is being heard nationally, that they're tight enough as a group to delay touring so Mark will be home when his baby is born in two weeks, that my son is much happier even though the band is less "his" than Lifer was.

Derek stands beside me through the whole show. Neither of us order a second beer. We don't do anything but pay attention to the music for the seventy-five minute Breaking Benjamin performance. And when the two-song encore sends the crowd happily into the late summer midnight, I stand with my sons in the litter of this release party and let them celebrate, the two of them going all the way back to Aaron's first show with Seed, four fifteen-year-olds covering Pearl Jam and Stone Temple Pilots at the Middleburg Community Swimming Pool when somebody's mother had hired them for $50 to play for a birthday party.

There's a video of that performance in my basement. Aaron's hair is Greg Allman length, straight to his shoulders and flailing each time the wind catches it. The band spaces its four originals among the grunge covers, all of which sound passable. The lowlight, I remember, is when they try The Who's "Baba O'Reilly," and Matt, the singer, needs to have a vocal range he doesn't possess. "Teenage wasteland," he sings plaintively, his voice cracking, but all the young girls standing near the stage look up adoringly.

Throughout October and November, while Breaking Benjamin crisscrosses the country, pictures and fan responses and interviews spring up on the Internet. By now the shots of Aaron from shows in Milwaukee or Grand Rapids or Little Rock have a sameness about them. The fans, even though they always speak in superlatives, don't say anything I haven't heard since before Strangers With Candy turned into Driver. And the on-line interviewers rely so heavily on the stock material of old press releases that it feels like I've read every one of them before.

But I check every day, and finally there are pictures I print out, Aaron and Ben after a show in Indianapolis, first with Kid Rock, who looks as agreeably wasted as Aaron and Ben, and second, Aaron and Ben looking stupefied as a half-naked young woman lies seductively across their laps. "She's a stripper," Aaron says on the phone. "It's all for publicity. She gets some; we get some. You know." I examine the pictures again as we talk, pleased that Aaron looks uncomfortable in the pictures with the stripper. "It was a little weird," he adds. "And Kid Rock was cool."

But all of this Internet activity, regardless of its repetition, annotates their schedule: Breaking Benjamin with Epidemic (from sellout to "maybe thirty people there"); Breaking Benjamin with Blindside (more of the same); and finally, Breaking Benjamin opening for 3 Doors Down, a tour that takes them to bigger venues, the crowds measured by the thousand instead of the hundred.

Better yet, their sales begin to climb. And though they're nothing close to huge, hovering between #10 and #20 on the Heatseekers Chart, which leaves them just outside the overall Top 200, they're selling, on average five times as many CDs per week as Lifer did.

When Aaron's cell phone rings fifteen minutes into his first after-coming-off-tour visit, I start to sense that Christmas season 2002 will be different than the one we endured in 2001. Though the call is short and I can count exactly how many words Aaron says—One "What's up?" three "Yeahs," and one "Later"—Aaron's responses are assured as well as snappy.

"That was Larry," he says. "We sold 8,800 CDs this week."

"Good," I say.

"Yeah. Sales are going up even though we're four months out with the CD. That's real good."

We're opening presents in a few minutes, the last people on earth, I think, to do so, since we've let Christmas Eve and Christmas go by while we waited for him to get his off-road life together. "Larry calls every Wednesday and gives us sales numbers. It's Thursday this week because of Christmas."

"All in less than thirty seconds."

"There's no messing around with Larry. It's all good. He tells me what's up and then he says 'I have to call Elvis.' He's calling Ben next. That's what he calls him."

"Elvis?"

"Yeah. You know. Star time. It's Ben's band."

I nod, but Aaron is rolling now.

"You know, Corey never called us after the first two weeks Lifer was out. I had to call him. It sucked. And then all he did was talk about how things were in the works. The works? We were selling a thousand CDs a week when we went on tour. And then it got worse. Universal said it cost $7,000 a week to keep us on the road. What do you think they were thinking when we started selling six hundred copies a week?"

"That's behind you now," I say, calling up a platitude to shift attention to belated Christmas.

Aaron looks at me. "It costs twice that to keep this band on the road, Dad. We're doing just well enough to tread water. Sooner or later we'll need another sales spike to keep this churning."

It's a caution, but if self-assurance is a sign of success, Breaking Benjamin is doing well. Aaron is relaxed. After we open presents he goes out with Derek and comes home with a new tattoo, the Zoso symbol from Led Zeppelin IV inked on his shoulder just below Gavin's birthday. It's the first new tattoo he's ever displayed. The other three, all on his shoulders, were discovered in a sort of accidental retrospective on a hot, humid, shirtless day.

"You're getting close to idiot's territory with these," I say, and Aaron, instead of getting defensive, smiles.

"Where's that?" he says.

"Anyplace that can be seen when you have a shirt on."

Derek laughs. "You said the same thing about hair gel and goatees," he says, his nod toward me a declaration about my fashion. "You'll be the first one in the family to get a Breaking Benjamin tattoo."

"And an earring," Aaron says. "You need to lose that prejudice."

"I'm only prejudiced when the tattoos are on my children. Other people are welcome to a hundred."

Aaron hands me a folder full of color photographs. I can tell they follow the 3 Doors Down tour. "Alcatraz," Aaron says, when I can't identify what I see in one of the photos.

"The guys from 3 Doors Down," he says, when I ask who's with him in a photo because none of them look as if they would be members of a rock band. "Corey Taylor," he says, when I pause at another, and I think of Slipknot, try to remember what sort of mask Corey Taylor wore as the band sledge-hammered their heavy riffs. In the photo he looks like anybody who might visit with Aaron, returned to the more mainstream project Stone Sour. "He's cool," Aaron adds. "Larry has him, too."

Aaron is casual with all this now. The guys in the pictures are peers. When Lifer came off the road a year ago from playing with Cold and Dope, he didn't show me one photograph. He didn't tell me one story.

The day after New Year's Aaron is sitting in our kitchen again when Larry calls to inform him they've sold 12,900 CDs this week. It's their highest weekly total, getting 2003 off to a promising start. I do the math and know that they'll go past 100,000 next week, that driving into six figures is a modest but important achievement.

When I say it aloud, Aaron nods. "Yeah," he agrees, "it makes us a B band, one of those bands you've heard of but aren't quite headliners. It makes us a solid opening band. It's all about sales, Dad. Or you get dropped." He rattles off the names of a dozen bands Lifer and Breaking Benjamin have played with that have been dropped, finishing with Boiler Room, Isle of Que, Dope, and Epidemic.

"You just played with Epidemic," I say.

"It was like Lifer all over again, Dad. They were down to selling less than 200 CDs a week. They found out they were dropped while we were playing with them."

"I looked you up. "Polyamorous" was #66 for the year in Active Rock. It was #83 in Mainstream Rock."

Aaron picks up his cell phone and checks the number as it rings. "Where do you find these things?" he says.

My wife and I drive to Wilkes-Barre for the post-Christmas show. It's a lousy night, snow already flurrying, more promised on top of the leftovers from the Christmas storm. We park a quarter mile down the highway in a lot reserved for township vehicles. "Trust me," I tell her, "this will be a good idea when it comes time to leave and there's cars everywhere."

As if on cue, we pass a group of fans who are digging a car out of the snow exactly where I'd seen the fans sinking their car into the mud in the summer. Two cars, this time, side-by-side as if the drivers had pulled in simultaneously, pleased with parking so close until they felt themselves settle deeply into snow that anyone could see was frame-deep from bumper-to-bumper. The fans had one shovel between them, and it was being wielded by a cursing twenty-year-old with a shaved head. "Fuck this," he shouted with each lift of the shovel. "Fuck this shit."

Inside, the club is nearly full even though there are two bands left to play before Breaking Benjamin goes on. I wait in line for a beer behind a guy who sports a scorpion tattoo that runs across the back of his neck as if it means to sink its poison into his throat.

And when I turn, beer in hand, to assess the room, I notice a group of six girls who all wear equally low-riding jeans, each of their lower backs showing a tattoo designed to dive into the waistbands of whatever they're wearing. All that's left to do is estimate the length of those crosses and zodiac signs, where exactly the last bit of ink resides.

Upstairs, Liz wanders into the area where the "band family" has blocked off space overlooking the stage. She sits at a table, settling in to talk to the wives and girlfriends, but I stay centered, watching Good Grief, an early band, because Tony is the drummer. They're a three-piece, playing all originals, as far as I can tell, because I don't recognize any of the songs. The audience is giving them a split decision, and so am I, impressed by how tight they are, what a solid drummer Tony is, but unable to hear the sort of hook that would make a crowd go crazy.

Two beers later, just after the last opening band finishes its set, Butch lets me cut into the men's room line, one that looks like those lengthy queues you see outside women's rooms. By the time we creep up and reach a space just inside the door, I see why. There are two urinals and one sink. I have more fixtures in my house. "That sink will be used," I say.

Butch smiles, then nods at the large blue wastebasket. "This, too," he says.

Across from that sink, at eye level, is a poster advertising an upcoming show by Lifer. "You going to be there?" I ask, pointing.

"I'm done stage diving," Butch says. "I'm getting married."

During the twenty minutes left before Breaking Benjamin's set, there's a reunion of sorts. Betty Jo and her friends are crowded against the railing of the balcony that looks directly down on the stage. Laura shows me snapshots of Gavin and her three-month-old daughter, the two of them posed together for Christmas. Her daughter is wearing a Bob Marley shirt, a gift from Aaron that acknowledges Mark's love of Reggae. Gavin, at seventeen months, looks huge for once.

Butch weaves in and out of the unofficial band-family vantage point. I find out his brother is the drummer for Cyphilis, who are here to open again with a forty-minute set of heavy rap metal. Aaron has told me the woman Butch is engaged to is Mark's sister.

It's an odd network, as if the bands themselves were tight neighborhoods where proximity made it likely couples might fall in love, where those who lived in or near these bands "stayed home" like young people did growing up a hundred years ago.

In this short amount of time I have two more beers bought for me by people I recognize and talk to, but whose names I can't keep straight. Three years of showing up once or twice a month, and I've remained simply "Aaron's Dad," though tonight, when Hyland introduces me to a huge guy going to fat, he says, "He's an icon" so easily I know he's said this before about me.

So I'm at home in this world where if I walked into any other show of its kind performed by another band I'd be looked at with surprise, suspicion, or worse. Here, when Hyland adds, "He's a writing professor," the enormous guy laughs and says, "That was a D course" and takes a long pull on his bottle of beer.

Two bras get thrown on stage early, giving Ben a chance to banter with the oversold room, but then there's a flurry in the crowd two rows back from where the bouncers stand behind the fence that keeps a narrow moat between the crowd and the stage. A bouncer leans forward, reaching, and then whoever it is who's out of hand tries to drag the bouncer over the front row, pulling and punching and making me think "really bad call."

Instantly there are four bouncers zipping through the crowd

from all the principal compass points, converging at a spot where the fan with no good judgment goes immediately down. The crowd parts, and those who don't step aside get slapped and kicked like tree branches hanging in front of an angry bear. The flailing fan is going out feet first, slammed, finally, into Larry, the manager, spinning him into the wall.

It's a moment that passes quickly, the next song roaring out over the crowd. Only Larry is assessing himself (later, he would say, "I took one for the team"), and though I'm certain this fan, because he attacked a bouncer, is being beaten outside, there's an unspoken consensus that he asked for it.

When I scan the crowd again I notice Tony has slipped into the no-man's land at the feet of the bouncers, who act as if he's a professional photographer, letting him walk back and forth with a video camera. He has the hood of his black sweatshirt pulled up over his head, but he looks more troll-like than urban-tough. And then, even more surreal, I notice that three of the four bouncers sitting on the stage are singing along with Breaking Benjamin, mouthing the words like middle school girls.

Despite his claim that he's retired, Butch walks out on the stage when "Sugarcoat," the band's heaviest song, begins. The song is punctuated by throaty screams from Ben, and the crowd is anticipating, their arms raised each time Ben roars, until, finally, Butch rocks back and then takes two quick strides and leaps, rolling onto his back and disappearing when the carpet of hands suddenly sags, making me think for a moment that he might have become the guy who took one jump too many.

Everybody around me leans forward, the railing feels mushy under my hands, and then Butch scrambles to his feet, coming up to mosh. A moment later half the crowd is swarming in spontaneous pits. Everybody knows that this is the last song, and a sort of desperation for chaos takes over, thick-necked guys spreading out and getting a running start into the center of whirlpools. The bouncers aren't singing now, but they let it go. For sure, there will be an encore. Nobody wants this to end.

Walking across the floor after I make my way downstairs five minutes after the show blinks out I crunch on a litter of broken glass and remember the moshers who fell. Derek is beside me, and by now the room is nearly empty, the bouncers working the crowd toward the exits. Tony has slipped the hood of his sweatshirt back down; beside him is Chris, putting four members of the original Lifer within a few feet of each other.

It's an odd moment, broken glass under our feet, each of our movements broadcast by a crunch. If this were a show of nerve, the quietest feet would win.

Ben walks over, greeted by "Star Hottie" and "Hottie of the Week." Everybody seems to know his picture is in *The Star* this week under the caption "Star Hottie." He blushes, but he gives in and pulls out a copy of *The Star* from the bag he's carrying.

The tabloid has made him look like an accounting major, somebody who will put on a tie in the morning and report early for work. If he walked past ten girls who were looking at this photo in a town 100 miles from here, none of them would scream "It's the Star Hottie!" as he passed.

The camaraderie here, the joking relentless, is refreshing. A year since Aaron joined, this is all still new and promising. A few days before, for the first time since Aaron quit the band, all the members of Lifer were in the same room, at a New Year's party at Club Xcess. Which really means Nick and Aaron were finally in the same room in public. Nick and his girlfriend, Beverly, were still together, lasting all the way from Strangers With Candy days. Like an extended family, everyone was taking pictures. "It was all cool until it got late and stupid," Aaron had said, and I hadn't asked him to elaborate

I decide to use the men's room before I leave, and Derek is inside, thinking the same way. The Lifer posters have been stolen from the wall. Derek points to the wastebasket. "Stay clear of that," he says, and I see it's so nearly full of urine I can't imagine how anyone will be able to do anything but tip it over and run, waiting for a night's worth of beer piss to slosh into every corner before the unlucky maintenance man slips back in to begin the thankless work of after-hours.

Just before I walk outside to see if it's stopped snowing in time to keep the ninety-mile drive from being nightmarish, I shake Butch's hand, rub his Marine Corps cut, and smile. It seems like a tangible period at the end of a long, convoluted sentence.

The road stories, even though Aaron offers them more readily now, are, in fact, more boring than the ones he's told about Lifer. Or at least more conventional: Jeremy's habit of always having three packs of cigarettes on hand, each pack a different brand. The band being listed as the sexiest men in Wilkes-Barre. The road manager having the evocative name of Joe Stumpo and being fired after one tour because he had "problems." Ben being a video game freak. The band threatened by a lawsuit because Ben sips from a can of Budweiser on stage in front of representatives of their sponsor, Miller Lite.

"Ben is Ben," Aaron repeats every time Ben appears in a story. "He does what he does."

Which is no help at all, except that I know Aaron's unhappy about something. "I'd rather be home with Gavin," he says. "Being a father's more important than this. And Mark's all about being into Laura and his baby. It's cool and not so cool at the same time out here. We're all about the music, not the lifestyle."

And though it fits the four of them well, this summary sounds so much like one of those lines a P.R. expert would spin into a recurring blurb that I'm tempted not to quote him.

By now I realize I'm seeing Breaking Benjamin differently than I did Lifer. I'm listening like a radio station program director, evaluating songs by their potential popularity. It's a lousy thing to do, and a hard thing to shake. "Under the radar" is a phrase I encounter over and over, not only in *The Album Network,* to describe bands and music invested in but infrequently heard. Like all of the arts, music is an iceberg business, with nearly all of the things that produce success being done out of sight. And more telling, nearly all of the performers spend their careers beneath the surface. "The average lifespan of a signed band is one and a half years," Aaron tells me. "Think about it. That means Lifer was average."

When I see the football coach at my university I ask him if he knows the average lifespan of an NFL player's career. "3.7 years," he says at once, the figure spoken so readily I understand he uses it as a caution even among the Division III players he coaches.

I'm convinced "Medicate" is the song with the most potential to be a major hit, and the band agrees, but the label decides on "Skin," the track on the CD that sounds most like a pop record. For a week I play the song each time I get in the car, trying to hear it like a teenager, listening for whatever it is that makes somebody call a radio station because she just has to hear it again, and when that's not enough, make her walk out of the mall with the whole CD in a record store bag. "Okay," I tell myself, but at least five other songs on the CD seem like better choices.

I want to see Breaking Benjamin on tour, how they are received when they're an opening band, and by the end of January I get my chance when their tour with Brand New Sin, Greenwheel, and Saliva comes to the Crowbar in State College. In the same club where I watched them open in front of a handful of people for a cover band a year ago and saw Lifer perform for an indifferent crowd fifteen months before, I'm relieved when Breaking Benjamin, playing third, is the best-received band of the night. And then I'm reminded that the Crowbar is close enough to home that this show may simulate the response I've seen over and over again in Wilkes-Barre.

"It's like a class reunion," Aaron says afterward. "There's guys here I haven't seen since the day I got a diploma."

"Good," I try.

"Yeah," he says, "good, but also amazing. There's even the guy who promised to punch my lights out when I took his old girlfriend to the prom."

"I'm sure that's slipped his mind by now."

"Don't count on it. It's just filed under irrelevant until he forgets I'm in a band."

He tells me that Food Dude ghosts have materialized. Girls who worked at Pizza Hut when he was a delivery boy. "They're still there," Aaron says. "I didn't think anybody kept a job like that for seven years."

What I remember from Aaron's months as a Food Dude delivery driver is how the manager of the KFC where he was based was shot in the head by a classmate of Aaron's, who said later, according to another classmate, "I capped the bitch."

Aaron had checked out minutes before the manager had walked out the back door with the day's receipts. That armed robber had worked there months before; he knew her routine. There was a chance he was already in his place of ambush when Aaron walked out without a bag of money, climbed into his truck, and drove home.

The woman lived, permanently disabled; the gunman-classmate was caught within days because he bragged about his robbery, finally, to someone who turned him in. Two weeks later Aaron would drive that truck to Orlando to begin music engineering school. It was Super Bowl Sunday. The roads were nearly empty, he told us later, for half the trip. He was calling from Florida because he hadn't stopped at a motel like we'd asked him to, driving straight through, 1,000 miles accompanied, back then, by only one guitar.

That afternoon I had looked up the picture of the local gangster in Aaron's old high school yearbooks. I followed his photographs through all four years, and there was nothing about them that suggested wannabe killer. "I never heard you say a word about this guy," I said to Aaron on the phone the night he arrived in Florida.

"He was just a guy who was there but not there," he said. "You know. He'd be at parties, but he'd be the guy sitting by himself. I didn't get into him at all. He was a pumping iron dude."

Shortly after the Crowbar show I turn on the television to a new sitcom called *Eight Simple Rules for Dating My Teenage Daughter*. "They're going to play "Polyamorous" during a party scene," Aaron had told me a few hours earlier when he called from the road.

I haven't watched a sitcom in years. In this one the dialogue is a series of one-liners followed by outbursts of what sounds like canned laughter. Nothing strikes me as funny, but when the teenage characters begin a series of exchanges that seem hilarious to the laugh track, I hear "Polyamorous" being played at a level so barely audible I want to tell the characters to either shut up or turn it up.

And then, finally, one character asks another to dance, something that seems unlikely to happen if "Polyamorous" were being played at a party, and for twenty seconds Breaking Benjamin is clearly heard in the homes of millions of viewers by an audience none of which I can imagine being over the age of seventeen.

And so there are "sightings." My wife hears "Polyamorous" on the tape loop at Foot Locker. *NHL Tonight* uses Breaking Benjamin when they run their Plays of the Week segment. And the video, occasionally played on MTV2, begins to appear more frequently, finally making the All Things Rock Countdown, working its way to #14 nearly five months after it was released to MTV.

Best of all, Melissa Joan Hart, who plays Sabrina the Teenage Witch, announces to millions of viewers of the American Music Awards that her favorite band is Breaking Benjamin. "How cool is that?" Aaron says. "And she and her boyfriend hung out with us. She came to our show in L.A."

All I can think of is Samantha, the original television witch, but I keep myself from boring Aaron with the distant pop-culture past. "She came up to Ben on the street," he goes on. "'Aren't you the dude from Breaking Benjamin?' she asked him. It was a good moment."

And now "Skin" shows up on the charts, moving from #112 to #42 in one week on Active Rock as it begins to go for adds. It's the start of campaigning again, as if another election were approaching, the record company stumping for votes like a presidential candidate going from market to market.

The song needs to do as well as "Polyamorous," and by the third week out it's more or less duplicating that success. Another three weeks of adds, I think, looking at the Mediabase charts on Tuesday, and it will be in the same territory. It's on forty-one of fifty-eight monitored stations in Active Rock; it's #30, and its ascent has slowed because the first fifteen songs or so have so many spins it's nearly impossible for Breaking Benjamin to get much past #19, the highest "Polyamorous" reached on the Billboard charts.

On Wednesday, although I already have a solid sense of what I'll see, I'll hold my breath and click the Radio and Records site to make certain Breaking Benjamin's position is, give or take two spots, the same as it is on Mediabase. And then on Thursday I'll click Billboard's Heatseekers chart and start to scan down, skidding toward disappointment once I reach #15 and they haven't appeared, panicked if I reach #25 (as far as the on-line version goes) and *Saturate* isn't listed, falling, I can calculate by that ranking, below 5,000 units scanned in the past week.

When I open one set of charts that lists, incredibly, the top 150, I see Lifer on Active Rock, #142, twelve spins, one station, and I think of hearing "Figment" while driving to the mall, the Wilkes-Barre station willing to play them despite the song coming out on an independent EP. And then I'm glad I didn't know about these charts when "Boring" went to radio, that I didn't click on to see it get to #70, with fifty spins across the country on seven or eight stations or something very close to that, bunched with songs by groups hardly anyone will remember because they've never had an opportunity to be heard.

On Mediabase, it turns out, I can follow the progress of "Skin" by the half day because it updates every twelve hours. It's astonishing what technology has done to this industry. Everything is scanned. Everything is fed to some central location where the numbers churn. Everything is designed to keep someone as obsessed as I am overinformed.

But what I also learn is that any sort of examination of station play lists demonstrates the state of the industry. The singles on these charts look like the arrangement of stores in the malls of America. A song that has the heavy rotation of thirty-six spins on one active rock station in Tennessee is almost certain to have more than thirty spins on an active rock station in Michigan. The twenty most played songs on those two stations match, with no more than two exceptions, the twenty most played songs on active rock stations in Texas and Missouri.

Finally, after I click on Breaking Benjamin's name on the Mediabase chart, I discover the full list of every radio station in the top 200 markets that plays "Skin" in a given week. Now, in March, there are 115 stations playing the song this week. Not surprisingly, nearly every station listed is playing the song in moderate rotation, between twelve and eighteen times per week, so I take note of the Columbus station that has them at thirty-seven spins and the three stations listed as zero, the song's absence recorded here because those stations played "Skin" once the week before and have apparently decided not to add it to the play list.

I think about some disc jockey simply playing the song because he likes it, a practice unheard of anymore. I picture him being fired for playing it because it's not on the list. I remember the fall semester of 2001, my wife calling my campus radio station to request "Boring" when the student disc jockeys asked for requests. "Sure," each of them replied. "We'll get it on." And then, without exception, it was never played.

I told Liz to stop calling. I found one of the students I knew who worked at the radio station and owned a Lifer CD herself. "What's the story with the request line?" I asked her.

"I can't play Lifer," she said. "They're not on our play list. I'll get fired if I do."

Fired? From a volunteer job? I think of college stations adhering to formatted play lists, somehow losing sight of their independence. Twenty years ago I'd been a disc jockey on that campus station, doing three-hour shifts on breaks and in the summer on the condition I could play whatever pleased me four times per hour, a dozen songs I could choose from the thousands of albums stored on shelves that filled three rooms. I tried new record after new record, testing songs on the second turntable while the other one sent music over the air. It didn't take long to discover a stack of records I loved, and as a result

I played songs I never heard on the radio again by Mink DeVille, Romeo Void, and The Brains, whose song "Electronic Eden" was my favorite cut to play for months. I think of The Brains showing up on a chart like this, one station, one play, and then, because a college radio station couldn't possibly be included here, I think of no hits at all coming up for The Brains except in my memory and on the tape I occasionally punch in when I'm driving by myself.

Only near the bottom of those play lists, down among the songs played once a day or less, can something dissimilar be found. A local band. A national band that is getting minimal airplay because it's on a label that doesn't have the resources to receive attention. A band that doesn't fit the established format. The bands, ultimately, that end up listed under L and B instead of being in a slot marked Lifer and Breaking Benjamin. A band whose sales rank on Amazon.com is 86,775. Or lower.

In the record industry, these groups might as well be poets. The highest ranking on Amazon.com for any of my collections of poetry has been 737,000.

There are worse numbers to be had. Currently six other listed books of mine trickle down to an astonishing 2,300,000. I feel like my next lowest ranking will mimic, without the decimal point, the place numbers in a computer-generated search for pi, but the last three books listed by publication date simply have no number whatsoever, meaning, I'm sure, that Amazon.com has never sold one copy.

So I click on Lifer, down to 59,668. And I learn that Sinch, a band that released its CD almost simultaneously with Breaking Benjamin has slipped below 60,000 already. "I think they're being dropped by their label," Aaron says, even though only eight months has gone by since their CD's release. As if the show has been scheduled by the demons of rock and roll, Lifer's website advertises that they're playing a gig with Sinch in Philadelphia.

Stop it, I say to myself, restricting my glances at Amazon.com to twice a day, Breaking Benjamin climbing as high as 400 and falling as low as 3,300, every ranking for eight months now higher than the best number Lifer ever reached. I've never had to refrain from checking the numbers for my books; for products ranked that low Amazon.com adjusts rankings once a month or less, not every hour.

After one of my sessions with Mediabase I tell Aaron, "I haven't seen any sign of Brand New Sin's first single."

"You won't."

I remember how I'd given myself up to their performance. The band had looked like a biker gang on steroids. They'd played full-throated, straight-ahead rock and roll that was appealing because it had no pretense. "They were signed, right?"

"Yeah, but it was with Now or Never Records. The same label that made us an offer. They're pretty small. They're signed, but that's the easy part. You need muscle behind a single."

"Payola?"

"Nothing's that simple anymore, Dad. Muscle is more sophisticated these days. Somebody might be out there with a wad of cash, but mostly it's all these favors you do for radio stations. You're out there promoting. It's all legitimate, but there's a system. We do these radio shows. We get our asses dragged out of bed real early. It's all cool once we're at the station, but you need to do these things to give yourself an edge if nobody's ever heard of you. You want somebody to be thinking about jacking up your spins. You show up. Or better yet, do a show promoted by the station. Bands play these for free, Dad. Everybody knows what's up."

I think *quid pro quo,* something harder to prove than direct cash payment. I think Alan Freed. None of this surprises me. "Brand New Sin were okay guys," Aaron goes on. "They're who they are, and they really get into it, but it's hard enough to make it even with Hollywood behind us"

Up Late

As the videotape of Great White's show at The Station begins, the Rhode Island club looks eerily familiar, so much like half the clubs I've watched Aaron play in during the past three years that I feel like reaching for my inhaler because I know how the low ceiling would trap smoke. I remember Great White's biggest hit, a cover of "Once Bitten, Twice Shy," but like everyone watching this tape being replayed on television news shows I'm paying attention to the pyrotechnics they're using, something like oversized sparklers showering sparks as they begin playing.

I've read the list of venues Great White visited in the weeks just before they played The Station. Breaking Benjamin played in The Stone Pony two months ago; Lifer played Crocodile Rock. "Using pyro in places like that is crazy," Aaron says, and nobody watching this film like we are would argue. Those white hot sparks set the back wall on fire; the flames run up to the roof and spread so rapidly it's as if the ceiling has exploded before the camera shuts off.

Aaron seems thoroughly spooked. "This is real bad, Dad," he says. "Do you see this guy here, the owner of the Stone Pony? I bet he knows somebody fucked up bad. Even you would know they had pyro if you were there. You don't miss something like that."

I switch channels to see if we can watch the tape again, remembering it's been nearly three years to the day since I first watched Aaron play in a club after the MTV career-launcher. More telling, I recall how I watched from that boxcar filled with piles of flammable trash.

When I first heard of this disaster I nearly held my breath while I waited to learn the name of the band that was playing at the time. I felt as if I was listening for a post-crash flight number when one of my children was in the air.

Now, watching the videotape a second time, I check to see which member of the band first notices the flames. It looks to me as if it's the guitar player I know is dead. "Lifer uses pyro," Aaron says. "It makes you think."

Suddenly even the arrangement of candles Breaking Benjamin used in their recent local shows seems dangerous, as if one of them could tip over exactly where the most flammable material is hanging. Suddenly rock and roll seems threatening, all of the stupid behavior and overcrowding nearly guaranteeing disaster. I know that there have been dozens of times that I've stood pressed among a thousand people at a show, twenty or more rows of fans between me and the main exit, the locations of any other way out nothing I'd given a thought to.

The third time we watch the videotape I scan the crowd. A few beer bottles are held aloft in salute. The fans near the front rock in place. This far into the film the back wall is already on fire. A fan in the second row raises a fist in what looks like appreciation.

One man finally turns toward the camera and gestures toward where the door must be. Two more fans turn as the flames reach the roof, and then the camera shuts off, the man doing the filming, I'm sure, heading for that door because he is listed as one of the survivors.

That low ceiling, we learn, had been soundproofed with cheap insulation that not only is highly flammable but also produces dense, toxic smoke that roiled out into the room so thoroughly poisonous those fans had maybe a minute altogether before the odds were they were going to die.

The fourth time I start to watch the film Aaron says "Enough," but I focus on the man in the crowd who appears to be oldest. He's near the back. He's not bouncing in place. But when that film ends, even as some people move past him, he still hasn't turned to rush toward the door.

For the first time since I was in high school I turn on the television after midnight. Already it's nearly 1 A.M., and I try to watch Conan O'Brien, but nothing about the conversation registers. I count how many times he picks up a mug that sits on the desk in front of him. I get to five in twenty minutes, but I probably miss some because I switch to Craig Kilborn each time commercials come on, and then I switch back, the mug already being raised to O'Brien's lips, put down, raised again, until I hear him begin to promote his "musical guest," and I know this is nearly over because Aaron has told me the guest band always comes on last unless they're huge. "The Ataris," O'Brien finally proclaims, and when they begin to play they sound so dreadful I start to worry that Breaking Benjamin, scheduled tonight on the Carson Daly Show, is about to reveal some profound musical weakness on network television.

To my dismay, this night's Carson Daly is an hour-long version of the usual half-hour show, and it's likely that Breaking Benjamin won't be on until after 2 A.M. Time begins to slow as if I'm a marathon dancer entering his second week. The only reassurance is the playing of Breaking Benjamin snippets as commercial lead-ins and Jeremy's drum kit set up in the background, visible throughout each interminable interview. This is late, late, late television where one set fits all.

And finally, at 2:05 Breaking Benjamin comes on to screams of approval—*NBC,* I think, and I lean forward as if Elvis has just stepped up to the mike on the Ed Sullivan Show.

After a month "Skin" has reached #25 in active rock, #30 in mainstream rock, and #35 in alternative rock. It looks as if it will duplicate the peak spins of "Polyamorous," but sales haven't spiked again despite an ad campaign that features a naked female torso that stops, top and bottom, exactly where the outermost limits of censorship begin.

What brings me back to these numbers more frequently again is the Album Network web site adding a "building" chart to its account of spins per week. Now I can track the number of spins "Skin" receives day-by-day in four different formats—Active Rock, Mainstream Rock, Alternative, and even Modern Pop, where, astonishingly, enough stations are playing "Skin" to chart it at #108.

One day. Two days. Three days. I slog on, and then after an entire seven-day cycle, I take a vow not to return to this information, that I can make do with one visit to the weekly total every Tuesday. And so far, a week later, I've kept to that diet.

Aaron looks puzzled when I confess to my habits. "I guess it's part of my book research," I say, but he's not convinced.

"You know more about Breaking Benjamin than I do," Aaron says, and I don't doubt it. Not only does he never look at the official web site, he doesn't see the on-line reviews, the promotions, and all of the format charts I follow. "You're taking this way too seriously," he says. "I bet even Larry isn't checking up on our spins every day."

"Who's been your favorite band to tour with?" I ask the afternoon I try to sort out Aaron's income tax calculations before he leaves for the Jagermeister Tour—Saliva, (hed) PE, Systematic, and Stereomud—in early March.

"3 Doors Down," he says at once. "They were cool with us."

The income tax payment he's going to owe looms as large as the fine paid by NBA players who bump referees. In this business nothing is withheld from the checks you receive. You think ahead or you have no way to pay. I try to imagine all the bands I've seen in the past three years putting aside about 25 percent of their income to cover themselves, but the lineup looks small.

Fortunately Aaron has done just that, but still he's saddened by the lump sum about to disappear without anything tangible in exchange. "What makes them different?" I ask.

"First off, they talked to us. I've toured with bands that didn't give any respect at all. I've toured twice with Saliva, and they don't even make eye contact. Lifer toured with Cold, and they just blew us off, but 3 Doors Down listened to our music and hung out. They were regular guys."

Aaron looks anxiously at the numbers I print on the itemized deduction form. Jeremy and Mark have had their taxes prepared by experts, and he knows how much they owed. "They had two buses, smoking and non-smoking. They let me sleep on the non-smoking bus some nights because it gave me a break from all the smoke on ours."

I show him what I'm adding together and where those numbers go on the main form. "And they gave us stuff when the tour ended. Band stuff, you know, hats and shirts and even a big bottle of vodka. The only words Josey Scott said to us on this last tour were, "You got any hard liquor?" He came up the stairs of our bus one night and shouted back to us, and when somebody said 'No' he disappeared. That's it. For the whole tour. I kid you not. What the hell? And Saliva's

out there rolling a lot of tape. Are you sure we've thought of everything I can claim as a deduction?"

"Probably," I say, but then, not wanting to let this go, I add, "What
do you mean, roll tape?"

"You know. Bands roll tape during their show to fill in things they
can't do on stage. Extra percussion. More guitar layers. We don't. We
are what we are, but sometimes you think you should because the
average fan doesn't even know that you're using a safety net.
Remember when Lifer played with Disturbed and they didn't come
on for over an hour? That's because their equipment overheated and
they couldn't roll tape. They wouldn't go on without it. And Saliva?
There's even back-up vocals on their tape. When you hear 'Click, Click,
Boom' those back-up mikes are dead. All the other guys have to do is
mouth the words. Josey Scott's doing all the work. And nobody in the
crowd gives a shit. If you're huge like they are, the crowd's not even
listening. They're just being there."

I put the unpromising tax forms aside and sit back. "You meet
many guys out there who see this world like you do?" I ask.

"No," Aaron says, "but I could be wrong. They don't know I'm
thinking like this. I go with the flow. I'm doing a job. I'm just lucky
enough to be doing something I'm good at and love. Rock and roll is
just being able to hear that something that makes people want to listen. You don't have to be perfect. Jimi Hendrix isn't perfect by a long
shot, but he had that something. I listen to classical music, and I don't
hear it as something I do. They're so much better technically than I
am that I don't even think about myself like that. What I can do is
play rock guitar, and what I've learned to have is stage presence."

"What group that you've played with are the best musicians?"

"Stereomud," Aaron says at once. "They're real good at what
they do."

"Who's bad?"

Aaron shrugs. "There's lots of bad. I guess Dope."

When he trails off, going silent, I know he's not going to elaborate on "bad."

"You might like this," Aaron says then, rewinding a videotape that
turns out to be something like one of those MTV The Making of the
Video shows. Laura, it turns out, filmed more than an hour of footage
during the video shoot for "Polyamorous."

We watch makeup sessions, director's decisions, instructions
about where to stand, where to look, how to move. It's the stuff of

rehearsals going to tedium. "More energy," Aaron says. "That's what Gregory Dark kept saying to me. Everything needs to be exaggerated for television."

"All of this," I say, "and then it was scrapped. It seems like such a bad call now. Who cares about the game *Run Like Hell?*"

"Nobody," Aaron says at once, though I'm sure he has no more idea about the sales figures for video games than I do.

"I looked for it once," I say, "in one of those stores that's all computer stuff."

"You got me beat there."

"There's so many games," I say. "Who plays them?"

"The same people who might buy our CD according to the record company."

The video finally arrives at what looks to be the final shooting sequences. "It was cool and boring at the same time," Aaron says. "And there was a lot of money wasted on paying people who had nothing to do."

I follow Gregory Dark, imagine him directing actors and actresses in the intricacies of porn. Here the sex is suggested rather than realized. "He was cool," Aaron says. "He knew what was up."

Over and over the band lip-synchs in the emptied swimming pool, and then, true to Aaron's original recounting, I hear Gregory Dark advise, "More energy."

"Check this part out," Aaron says. "The neighbors called the cops. That's what's going on here. Too much noise, they said. We had to turn everything down. It sort of sucked because it made it harder to be energetic."

Finally, though, watching the video being made is depressing because it won't be seen. It's as if the band and people close to the band like I am own the director's cut of the video. And in this case, a few minutes of additional footage is enormous because the video is only three minutes long.

A week later my wife and I drive to Washington, D.C., to see the third stop on the Jagermeister tour. The Nation, the club where the show is, looks like a larger version of The Staircase, and at first glance the faces look the same, everybody, because it's an all-ages show, seemingly between sixteen and twenty-five.

The difference is the buzz. Instead of the whole crowd pressing forward, maybe 70 percent does, so there are gaps here and there, spaces where someone could stand untouched without being in the very back. Even within two minutes of the beginning of Breaking Benjamin's set there are a hundred people at the bar, a hundred more standing nearby talking as if they were at a party in someone's living room.

My wife and I hurry upstairs, make our way along a balcony until we're near the right side of the stage. It's where Liz loves to stand, a lousy spot for sound quality, a great spot for watching Aaron, who is always to the left side of the stage. She settles against the railing, and I look past her for an Exit sign. Not seeing one, I check behind us, note the location of a set of stairs leading down to where the air would be better if smoke filled this room. I don't say anything to Liz.

When the Wizard of Oz soundtrack begins, the "I'll get you my pretty" lines cackling out of a mix of swirling sound, the part of the crowd that screams for "Home," as if this were a Beatles show, is nearly all girls. I'm happy, after a few songs, to see a pit form; half the guys who are flailing and shoving have stripped to the waist like football fans. They look beefier than the Wilkes-Barre moshers. I almost expect huge letters painted on their chests, a pit that spells out BREAKING BENJAMIN if it somehow arranges itself in the proper order.

At this show, though, the frantic rocking in place of the girls in the crowd seems more animated than the action in the pit. They fling themselves into the music, hair tossing, the sort of abandon that fuels sex fantasies. Their boyfriends, for the most part, are impassive, and I understand that they've come for bands far heavier than Breaking Benjamin, that, in fact, Lifer would do better here, that a dose of "Heave" and its call to arms of "So get the fuck up" would rouse more of them than the pop hook of "Skin."

After the show ends, the short set of seven songs and no encore evaporating like water spilled on a midsummer driveway, Liz and I walk toward the rear exits, one of which we'd entered forty minutes before with the band. Stopping backstage, I lean against a railing beside Mark, who's trying to cool down before he takes the hike between trailers and buses to where Breaking Benjamin's tour bus is parked. (hed) PE's crew is setting up, while a shirtless man who appears to be wearing a tattoo vest prepares for his between-acts performance. "That dude has his nose pierced so he can work a snake in and out of his head," Mark says. Looking at the man's lurid green face and arms, I don't doubt it. "He swallows all kinds of shit and brings it up and then drinks it," Mark adds. "He keeps the crowd busy for a few minutes between sets."

A boy about eight years old walks past as if this was the stage at the elementary school. He belongs, I guess, to somebody in (hed) PE, a funk/rap metal fusion band whose sound is a distant cousin to Breaking Benjamin's pop metal. I remember all those guys I'd noticed getting restless for something heavier. They'd raised hundreds of fists when Ben had shouted, "Are you ready for (hed) PE?" midway through Breaking Benjamin's set, more fists, in fact, than went up for Ben's reference to Saliva ten seconds later. And though the band members seem like reasonable people, the vocalist polite and soft-spoken when my wife asks him which back door will lead to Breaking Benjamin's bus, they all have the tattoos and piercings and spiked goatees that are calculated to endear the fringe and frighten the mainstream.

Aaron has already left the building, so Liz and I try to retrace our pre-show path, walking between buses that seem identical in the dark. There's no sign of girls trolling for rock stars. It's early March, dark and cold. We could as easily be climbing into a bus full of bedraggled cross-country travelers. If there are women prepared to offer themselves to my son, they're lying low. He's more likely to meet a mugger outside of this Washington, D.C., club than a groupie.

"Did it sound good?" Aaron asks at once when we're finally inside the tour bus. When I hesitate, explaining that we were standing to the side of the stage, he frowns. "So the mix sucked?"

"No. It's just that the bass seemed more prominent because of where we were standing."

"It's hard being the fourth band. You just go on and hope the sound isn't too bad when you start. You never know what's coming out on the first song."

"It was good," I hurry to say. "Don't worry."

Later, when we go back inside the club, Jeremy asks me the same question—"How did we sound?" And then Ben, two minutes afterward, repeats the exact same question. As always, nobody in the band asks, "How was the show?" or "How did we look?"

And each of them knows the answer before I speak, so it's not good enough to say "great" or "awesome." I need to refer to bass and treble, mix and timing, before I elaborate on crowd reaction.

For a couple of songs we all watch (hed) PE perform. The raps quickly get monotonous. In one song they are reduced to a "Fuck me" "Fuck you" call and response exchange between the front man and the guy working turntables. A few minutes later the band churns out a repeated chorus of "Everybody dies" as if they've just thought of it. But it's somehow infectious, and the band is working hard, generating a frantic crowd reaction, including, nearby, the fattest mosher I've ever seen.

Aaron notices him, too. "You don't see that every night," Aaron says. "A four-hundred-pound dude getting down."

We skid toward the back of the club, none of us following the final songs in the set. When I mention "Skin," Ben says, "The worst song on the record, and it's the second single."

I keep my agreement to myself, but I hazard my skepticism about the band merchandise prices.

Ben agrees. "I'm really pissed off about all this, but we have to live with it."

"We have to match prices," Aaron explains. "It sucks. Saliva can sell a shirt for $25, but we can't, not many at least. Or a hat for $30. What's up with that? Who would buy one?"

The singer from Systematic slides in beside Aaron to a series of "Hey mans" all around. "You guys rocked," I say at once, honestly giving a compliment. Of the other four bands, Systematic is the one I enjoy most tonight. In fact, of all the other signed bands I've heard play with Lifer and Breaking Benjamin, I like watching them best.

The singer smiles. His head is shaved except for sideburns that seem levitated, disconnected from him. I think for a moment they might be paste-ons, like a fake mustache turned vertical and applied just below his temples. He's polite, but there's no question he wants to hang out with Aaron and Ben.

So I wave them off and work my way through the crowd, getting into position just behind the bare-chested moshers so I can focus on the back-up mikes. I know "Click, Click, Boom" will be the first song in Saliva's set because Aaron has told me it's exactly the same as the set they played on tour with them during the winter. Within a minute or two I'll be able to see for myself how that chorus is handled.

I watch the guitarist to my left step up to the mike and mouth the words. It looks like he's singing, but the volume is so much louder than the other bands, everything has turned tinny. In fact, the band sounds artificial, so many layers of sound I know Aaron is right. I could sing back-up as long as I could remember the words "Click, Click, Boom."

What I can't tell is whether or not the guitarist could lift his fingers from the strings and be covered, but one song is enough to satisfy me. I go upstairs to the third-tier level, passing a security guard who barely slows me down when I say I'm with Breaking Benjamin.

There's food up here. Cold cuts. Baked ziti. Chips and pretzels and a view that makes me think *Phantom of the Opera, just before the masked organist swings down over the crowd.* The sound, this close, is deafening, even by rock and roll standards. My wife, between songs, wants to know what's up with Josey Scott's long, buttoned coat and the gloves he's wearing. I can only tell her it's the exact same outfit he wore six weeks before. And then I tell her it's the same set. Even the same phrases between songs, as if he's memorized a series of short speeches, the patter so canned it's as predictable as the language used in a tour of the White House a mile from where we stand.

"It's his persona," I finally say to Liz as Ben approaches to hand me a beer.

Ben smiles. "Yeah," he says. "It's like he's playing Josey Scott instead of being Josey Scott."

When they reach Albuquerque, Breaking Benjamin goes off tour to record a performance of "Skin" for the Craig Kilborn Show. *CBS,* I think, *another major network.* And though this program is another late, late show, it at least directly follows David Letterman, coming on at 12:30.

Because they're taping in Los Angeles, Shannon and David, who have moved there from New York, get tickets. Aaron flies Betty Jo out for what amounts to a three-day vacation. Laura and Yvette fly out as well, and the taping seems like a reunion.

When Aaron calls he's not as excited as I expected him to be. "We were better than we were on Carson Daly," he says, "but it was all pretty cheesy. Daly's live in front of the audience that's watching the rest of the show. Kilborn's taped in front of an audience that sees the show that's on that night live."

"What?"

"We're on in ten days, Dad. Shannon and David and Betty Jo saw us tape, but another band was shown on tape at the end of the show they saw. That's the way Kilborn does it. When you watch, you'll see him wave his arm toward the stage as if we're standing there, but we're not. We'll be in Seattle or someplace like that. It's not cool."

I sort through his explanation, thinking of nothing to say but, "That sounds sort of lame."

"We saw Craig Kilborn for two minutes. He came into the dressing room and said, 'Okay, whose hands do I have to shake?' and then he was out of there. The only thing that was said was when Ben looked at him and said, 'You're a tall motherfucker.' You know Ben. He's like six feet four or something, so Kilborn's big all right, but I don't think it went over that well."

The tour swings up the west coast, so the band's web site quiets down for a while until a message board argument breaks out about Breaking Benjamin covering a Tool song as an encore. "Tool is God," somebody writes. "This is sacrilege."

Breaking Benjamin fans rally, but another message pans the band, predicts it will soon disappear because it sounds like every band. A series of "Fuck yous" follows. I want to log on and tell them my son, aside from those times he has a guitar in his hand and it is plugged into an amp, is an unlikely rock and roller. He owns a house, and he's been more of a handyman in the year he's sporadically lived there than I have been in the thirty years I've owned four houses. He has a son he dotes on. He would think me an idiot for even considering trying to explain him to the host of teenage girls who dominate the message boards.

It's harmless, I say to myself. An outlet. It's attention, after all, whether it's praise or criticism. But they go on at length about which song should be the next single. They write treatments for each song they choose, not recognizing that it's unlikely Hollywood will invest more money in the band unless they somehow spike to 10,000 or more scans a week.

And then I feel foolish for even reading the messages, as if I'm a principal of a middle school eavesdropping on homeroom conversations. I stop logging on altogether for a week. All of this Internet activity is as depressing as listening to drunks arguing about sports at a bar, every beer swiller believing for a few hours that he absolutely knows what's best for his hometown team in baseball, football, or basketball.

And finally Aaron, when he calls, seems as depressed as he was in Lifer's last days. "Ben's being Ben again," Aaron says. "Four of us quit. Larry. Ripper. Mo. Me."

"Mo?"

"You know. He's been our sound man since forever."

"But you're still touring."

"Yeah. Ripper quit the most. I thought he still meant it the next day."

I wait until Aaron answers my unasked question. "It's just a bunch of stuff. There's no talking to Ben about promotions and stuff like that. Ben cancels radio shows. We do those to keep the spins up, you know, and then he blows them off. And there's nothing going on with him about my music. It's cool and it's not cool at the same time. Ben is so into his music he doesn't care about the rest of it."

I've listened to Aaron be way up and way down for four years, but this complaint seems really crucial to resolve. "Yes, he does. Ben knows he can't do this by himself."

"You talk to him," Aaron says. "You need to hear his side of things and see what you think."

And so I do, calling Ben's cell phone number to get a better idea of what "Ben is Ben" means, beginning to leave my name when he picks up, so I know he screens his calls.

"You okay with this?" I say at once. "I have some easy questions, but there are some hard ones, too. You know how things are sometimes shaky."

I feel like I'm apologizing, that I'm turning into a rotten reporter because I can't divorce myself from my feelings about my son, but Ben sounds at ease. "I'm okay with it," he says. "No problem."

I start with his fear of flying and the hypnotism experiment. "You have to be willing in order to be hypnotized," Ben says at once. "I don't want to fly, so I didn't want to be hypnotized into thinking it's okay. The label put me up in a hotel for a week. It wasn't like it is in the movies. They had me lay down and focus on a light on the wall. They tried to make suggestions during that time right before you fall asleep, but I wasn't having it."

I remember the long, last section of *Ulysses,* how Molly Bloom's mind spun out fifty pages worth of the extraordinary jumble of conscious and unconscious thoughts to end Joyce's novel. I keep my literary allusions to myself, remembering, as well, that Ben has promised to read this book even though, he claims, "I haven't read one since I was fifteen."

"And they tried media training on you, too, right?" I say, and Ben answers so quickly I begin to sense what "Ben is Ben" means. "This band is my business," he says. "I've been working at this since I was fourteen years old. Nobody has to tell me not to bad mouth other bands. I know that's a bad idea, but if I want to do it, I will."

"That can annoy people," I hazard.

"Sure it does. I know that, but I'm going to do what I need to do, not what somebody tells me to do."

Because it seems as if he has something else to add, I wait for a moment.

"The songs are what we are," he finally says. "The rest is bullshit. I've worked too hard to let somebody else tell me how to do this."

A moment passes like an agreement, and then I ask him about the first version of Breaking Benjamin, the one he left behind. "I went to California back then because I had a new direction I wanted to try. I had new songs, and the band, the way it was then, had gone as far as I thought it could. Chris and Nick Hoover were good, but Aaron was the only one I wanted to ever play with again."

"I heard those songs. Aaron played the tape."

"Really? That's cool. But you know what I mean? I only want to play with guys I want to play with. Jeremy's an awesome drummer. You don't find many drummers who can create excellent drum hooks. And Mark's the best bass player in the area. When he joined I knew we had something. And then Aaron came along again, and he's the only guitarist I'd add. It's perfect."

"So what did you think when you ended up opening for Lifer at their record release show. Was it hard listening to them when you knew you had all those songs?"

"I was very proud," Ben says immediately. "I'd played with Aaron and Chris. I've been friends with Aaron since whenever. I wasn't angry or anything like that, but sure, I was jealous."

"Okay," I say, relaxing. Listening to Ben has been like listening to a younger version of myself, somebody so convinced he knows what's best for what he loves that it keeps him from hearing others.

"So," Ben says, "are you going to make me sound like an idiot?"

"No," I say. "I understand." And saying that, I believe it, though even as I admire Ben's talent and single-mindedness, I can sense how "Ben is Ben" means perpetual conflict.

The day of the Kilborn show I discover a parody of "Poly-amorous" on a web site. "Hardly Glamorous" is its title, and it is so uninteresting I can't fathom someone taking the time to work out all the lyrics.

Another site features a contest for mock Breaking Benjamin CD covers, and to my astonishment nearly a hundred of them come scrolling down, about one out of four playing off a connection to Creed established in the very first entry, people borrowing their sense of the record from a picture rather than listening. These PhotoShop devotees likely haven't even heard the music, their creations something to do in order to be seen—like some sort of virtual support group for those with the latest software.

And now, incredibly, there's a Breaking Benjamin tribute band— The Kwintos Theory. They have a website. They're based in upstate New York, and the site advertises their CD release party for a compilation of Breaking Benjamin covers—*PolySaturated.*

It feels like lunacy, these things. And though, as always, Aaron turns upbeat again, smoothing things over with Ben, excited about performing, it's not surprising that he mentions his goal of getting off the road, putting touring behind him and settling into studio work. "Another year of this," he says. "Maybe two if it really takes off." And I know he sees giving up the road as something that will allow him to be a presence for his son, something that will encourage lasting relationships. The romance of celebrity lifestyle is just that, after all— romance. Something envied and wished for by those who don't live it because those people, the audiences for celebrity, witness only the joyful moments of performance and its immediate aftermath.

I'm not at all surprised. Even in the more modest world of literary writing, romance is attached to book publishing. Authors travel to read from their work. Authors appear on talk shows. And a few authors make fantastic sums of money. And then they go back to the isolated work of writing, driven by a self-discipline that often seems something like a low-fat diet or a years-long hiatus from alcohol, a habit to let go of.

Of all the nights to appear on Craig Kilborn, Breaking Benjamin is scheduled for April 7, an evening when CBS will delay its latenight programming because of the NCAA championship basketball game.

As soon as the game ends at 11:30 I'm relieved, telling myself it's only half an hour. And then, to my horror, a post-game show begins, complete with redundant interviews and determinedly poignant music that emphasizes the agony and ecstasy of the tournament so relentlessly it's as if a contemporary Michelangelo should choose college basketball as his subject for a twenty-first century Sistine Chapel.

I trudge upstairs to read, the television murmuring from the basement like polite guests who cannot sleep. At 1:30 I return to my chair, knowing the band won't perform until nearly 2:30, but hoping they will be mentioned or their music will be used as transitions to commercials.

So I hear "Next to Nothing" and then, after enduring guests who try to promote their current movies without sounding like the veg-o-matic guy, a thirty-second spot of the "Polyamorous" video plays, followed by Craig Kilborn holding up the CD and giving, I know, an expansive, upbeat intro to a band that isn't there.

The performance itself is anticlimactic. Aaron isn't miked for backup, something that I imagine brought on some of his unhappiness the week before. Jeremy is more animated than he was on Carson Daly. Ben's performance is more assured. The song ends, and I rush upstairs, see that it's 2:39, and sink into bed.

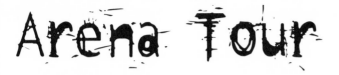

Arena Tour

Long live MyDownfall!!!!!! — bad attitude. a fan

"Everything's cool again," Aaron says when I call after Breaking Benjamin has been out with Godsmack for a few days.

"So Ben isn't Ben now?"

Aaron laughs. "No, he's always Ben, but we're talking about stuff and he's doing all the promos again. Dad, he's a genius song writer, and we'll always be friends."

I tell Aaron I'm about to drive ninety miles to see a Lifer show. "They call themselves MyDownfall now," I say. "Chris is comping me in." Because I want to keep it a surprise, I don't tell him Chris has hooked me up with the company that produces gold records for qualifying artists, that I've ordered him one because "Breathless" is on *The Scorpion King,* and the compilation has gone way past gold.

"Speaking of Lifer," Aaron says, "I got a royalty check the day we left. I have it right here. You want to know what it says?"

"Sure."

"It's unbelievable. Thirty-five dollars. For the whole year of 2002. The most spins we got was twenty for "Not Like You." Twenty spins in a year? And "Boring" got six spins. I wonder who played it?"

"So Chris and Nick won't be celebrating a big payday?"

"Here's something you'll like. "Breathless" is down for .8 spins on cable, whatever that means. What did they do, cut it off before it ended? .8? How lame is that?"

"You have stations that give you forty spins a week now, and you're still fighting for air."

"That's the truth. We're doing just good enough to stay out on tour. Systematic and Stereomud have been downgraded to RVs in order to stay out."

"RVs?"

"Yeah. Systematic's CD hadn't even come out yet, and their label kicked them out of their tour bus. They said their first single wasn't getting enough spins so they expected the CD to tank."

"I saw their spins on Mediabase. Half of what you're getting for "Skin." Maybe not even."

"There you go."

"I'm guessing you've gone past 150,000 scans by now."

"Yeah, right around there, but that might not cut it. We could be next. This Godsmack tour will tell the story about whether or not Hollywood will keep us on the road. If we don't sell at least 5,000 CDs every week, the label loses money on us."

"Lifer never sold 5,000 CDs in a week."

"Exactly. The record was so late coming out with all the name change bullshit that we didn't catch the wave. None of us knew how fast the label would throw in the towel. And then there was that whole cover-band thing we couldn't get past."

"If Strangers With Candy was still playing covers, what would you be covering now?" I ask.

"System of a Down probably," Aaron says at once, and then, "I don't know," and I can tell he doesn't want to consider returning to the old days.

"Disturbed," I say. "Drowning Pool. Mudvayne. Papa Roach."

"Stop," he says. "There's no way I would do Papa Roach."

"If people went nuts for "Last Resort," you'd play it every night."

"And that's why I'll never be in another cover band."

Two hours later, the first thing I notice walking into The Staircase is the air is so clear of cigarette smoke I can breathe without being apprehensive. Somewhere in Wilkes-Barre are thousands of old fans of Strangers With Candy, Driver, and Lifer who are doing something else this evening besides eyeballing the evolution of a band, but within seconds I see someone waving me over to the nearly empty bar. Hyland. He's sitting with EJ, Lifer's old soundman, and a couple of Yuengling Lagers. So I'm not without familiar company. When I scan the room, though, not one of the other hundred or so early arrivals looks like somebody to whom I can attach a name. No Strangers With Candy shirts. No Lifer shirts. The rock T-shirts in this crowd say System of a Down, Deftones, and Mudvayne.

Hyland wants to talk about a reunion show. "MyDownfall and Breaking Benjamin," he says. "That would fucking rock. Aaron and Mark could play with Chris and Nick. Everybody could be on stage together at the end. Tony, too. You know how many people would come to that?"

"An arena show," I say, adding *around here* to myself. Already this feels like a class reunion, a conversation with the first person who happens to recognize you after years away from reading *Hamlet* and doing trigonometry.

"Aaron called me," Hyland says. "It was all good."

I order a beer and click the bottle against his. "I'm glad," I say. And it feels like I'm back.

Agents of the Sun, a band from Baltimore, takes the stage. They seem young and nervous, and there aren't more than fifty people standing near the stage, the rest of the club gathered in small groups at tables or even shooting pool. But after two songs they pull things together and generate some attention. A solid band, I think, but it's hard to feel excited when half of the small crowd is sitting down.

I read "Terrorist Action Group" on the back of the T-shirt of a stranger who slides up beside Hyland and E.J. When he turns I see an automatic rifle pictured on the front. It hovers over the word AMEN, setting a tone for anyone within reading distance. I finish my beer and decide to go downstairs among the teenagers.

I don't manage ten steps before I have to slip past an enormous guy in shorts and a T-shirt that reads "Saddam Hussein 1937–2002." I wonder when he bought the XXXL shirt, whether there are 1937–2003 editions on the market, whether he will update if Saddam Hussein is found under the latest pile of rubble in Iraq.

Right behind him is Tony, the hood on his sweatshirt pulled down for once. "I saw you on the guest list," he says. "When are you coming to check out Good Grief?"

"I saw you guys at Christmas," I say. "Remember?"

Tony brightens. "Yeah, you did," he says, but then he sags. "But we sucked then, and now I heard you're finishing the book."

"I'll get Good Grief in the book," I say.

Tony lights up. "Good," he says, "but you need to hear us now so we don't suck in our part."

Downstairs, I walk right up to within ten feet of the stage, only two solid rows of teenagers in front of me. I haven't been this close to the stage since Strangers With Candy's pre-MTV days, and when

Agents of the Sun end their set, the applause and shouts remind me of those off-camera whoops I heard on old videotapes from the days before Tony joined the band.

Two guys from Agents of the Sun begin to work the room, carrying clipboards with lined paper, and I know they're trying to get names and addresses for a mailing list, talking up the fans one by one, saying "thanks" for each printed name, holding a handful of their self-produced CD and hoping someone will give them money as well as an address. "You guys rock," a girl says, and both guys beam. Behind them, up on the stage, the rest of the band is busy loading out.

Just before Cyphilis takes the stage, I notice Chris by the back door. For a moment, when I shake his hand, I feel awkward, a fan aged way past justifying being here. "Thanks for guesting me in," I say, sure of one opening line.

"No problem."

We run through the trivia of what's been happening and how things are. "The showcases didn't go anywhere, but Matt Pinfield is interested," Chris says. "You know who he is from MTV and stuff?"

"Yeah," I say, though "interested" sounds like a euphemism for "we met him."

"He's keeping his eye on us," Chris goes on.

I say "Good" to keep things going, and then Chris says, "The name thing coming up again is weird."

"Maybe you should go back to Strangers With Candy," I say, but Chris shakes his head.

"This one's all about Derek and Ian feeling like they're in the band. You know, as long as we're Lifer, there's more guys not there than in the room. Aaron and Mark and Tony are more about Lifer than Derek and Ian. We had to toss that shit and move on."

When Cyphilis comes on, all of them in identical black jumpsuits, there's no way to hear each other. Every song they play is full of heavy riffs and guttural choruses roared by their front man, who's as entertaining as ever, but I go upstairs to watch with the adults, move to the railing overlooking the stage, where a guy in all black turns and gives me a once-over. "You look familiar," he says.

"So do you," I say, and then, figuring it's the only possible reason, I add, "I'm Aaron's dad."

His smile is as broad as Tony's was. "I'm Ian," he says. "I used to have braids and all that."

"I remember. We met at that last Lifer show Aaron played."

"Yeah. It was tough back then, me being new and stuff." Ian smiles again. "How far is it for you to come to this?"

"Ninety miles."

Ian shakes his head. "Wow," he says. "I'm honored."

A few minutes before MyDownfall is about to go on, I can see that half the floor downstairs is still vacant. Even with the heavy set by Cyphilis, there hasn't been a mosh pit all night. The combination of space and no violence is an invitation to go back downstairs and watch the band from fifteen feet away. And so, when the strobes begin to flicker and the band walks onstage one by one to murmurs and squeals, I'm sufficiently close to be heard if I decide to yell "Fuck, yes!"

And Nick, as soon as the spotlight flares on, fills the room. He poses and struts. He gestures to the crowd to "give it up," and they do, screaming as loud as half a crowd can. There's no question, from first song to twelfth, that MyDownfall kicks ass.

Finally, the last two songs keep Nick's promise to "tear shit up." Nearly all the modest crowd presses forward, sensing a climax. The strobe lights go into a migraine-producing frenzy. And then the Cyphilis front man, looking almost ordinary in street clothes, steps out to join Nick in a give-and-take sing-and-scream on "Wake Up," the first song on MyDownfall's self-produced EP.

Derek, Aaron's replacement, repeats this latest riff as confidently as Aaron did Lifer's old ones. Ian seems as solid as Mark. They've reached the end of an hour-long show without playing one Lifer song.

"Opportunity knocked, but you walked away," Nick wails, and then they exchange "Listen to me!" each of them screaming the plea as if it might solve a lifetime's worth of problems.

I remember Aaron telling me the song is about him leaving the band, and nothing about the lyrics suggests otherwise. More than a year after he quit, though, it doesn't sound nearly as pointed. Now it's a crowd-pleaser, a way for Nick to suck the audience forward. And for these last few minutes of the show, I'm as taken in as I was when Aaron stood alongside him.

A minute after the band leaves the stage I stand among a dozen teenage girls who hold CDs or drumsticks or even copies of the article about MyDownfall in the Wilkes-Barre newspaper's Weekender section that was piled by the club door. They're as anxious and jittery as the Candy Girls were three years ago. There are just far fewer of them, and none of them move closer to the stage door than where Derek, the new guitarist, talks softly to them one at a time.

I think, *Santa Claus at the mall line,* a wish list of autographs and souvenirs and stories to tell friends at school tomorrow. When Ian steps out I slide forward and ask him if it's okay to go backstage, a request I haven't made in four years. "Sure," he says. "Nick and Chris are both there."

And when I open the door it's Nick, standing among guitar cases, who I see first. I read his smile as genuine, and I extend my hand. He pulls me into a hug, and I'm suddenly both relieved and happy. "You're still a great front man," I say, meaning it. "You guys rock."

"Thanks," he says, and we drop right into dialogue about MyDownfall, Lifer, Driver, and Strangers With Candy. Chris walks down the stage steps and sits on one of them beside where we stand.

"Yeah," Nick says. "I was really pissed when Aaron quit. Really pissed. But I'm over it."

"Good," I say.

"It's just that things were really going good when he left."

I give him a few seconds to elaborate, remembering nothing that was going good, remembering, too, that Aaron had told me the rest of the band somehow thought Lifer was on the verge of success despite selling 30,000 CDs in five months and having no tour dates scheduled for the next two months and counting. All they had to go on as 2002 began was that *The Scorpion King* was scheduled for release in February; if the band could fantasize "Breathless" being the second single from the compilation CD, following Godsmack's "I Stand Alone," they could imagine Lifer blowing up all over the country. It's just that Aaron couldn't.

"We saw each other when he was home in the winter," Nick says then.

"New Year's Eve," I offer.

"Yeah, but I was hammered."

"All Aaron said was 'It got stupid.' He never gives up the details. If Derek had been there I'd know exactly what was said and done. He's been telling me stuff about the old days, Hoover and his guns and all that."

"Hoover was a story all right," Nick says.

I feel like I'm getting collaboration, the second source of a conscientious journalist. "I've been hearing about Hoover bringing a gun to every show."

"And to practice," Nick says at once.

Chris nods. "Everywhere," he says. "That was Hoover."

"He still follows all the bands," I say.

"That's cool," Chris says. "It was just business that pushed him out of the band. I hope he has his shit together."

"Breaking Benjamin is the greatest band in the history of music."
— shallowbay, a fan

"Oh my gosh Breaking Benjamin was sooooooooooooooooo amazing!"
— polyamorous friend, a fan

"It's a nice day," Derek says as we approach the Utica Memorial Auditorium. "It's Godsmack. You can bet we'll see guys with their shirts off in line."

Sure enough, we total up more than twenty shirtless men as we creep past the line toward the parking lot after driving 270 miles to see an arena show. Though we don't count, there have to be a hundred or more tank tops on other men who stand among women who all seem to be wearing jeans that ride so low they slip toward the line of demarcation for gravity.

It's 6:30—doors-opening time. The lines begin to lurch forward. Breaking Benjamin goes on in an hour. Ten minutes later the two of us discover we have no idea how we're getting inside without the tickets we expect at the will-call window.

Fortunately, Ripper walks out from behind the auditorium and calls my name. He's in all-black, like a benevolent angel in camouflage, and we joke about how I didn't recognize him in State College in January after I'd met him less than a month before.

"But I know you now," I say, introducing him to Derek.

"We're getting laminates for both of you," he says. "You'll have access to everything except Sully's dressing room." I smile, knowing enough about Godsmack to recognize the singer's name, but Ripper's description comes in such a serious tone I begin to equate attitude with Sully.

We find our way to a dressing room marked Breaking Benjamin. It's 6:45, and yet only Jeremy is inside. "Aaron's running late," Ripper says. I nod, knowing Aaron has taken the off day between West Virginia and New York to spend at home planting shrubbery and spending time with Gavin and Betty Jo. "She's driving up with me to the show," he'd said. And then, in answer to my complaint about driving distance, "It's not that far."

"How late is late?" I ask.

"He's ten minutes out. He's got time."

I suddenly feel like a father. "I could have told him he didn't allow enough time," I say. "It's a hike up here, even from Wilkes-Barre."

Jeremy nods, but he hasn't stopped drumming on a chair since we've walked in. Thank God it's a padded seat, because there's no sign he's going to quit any time soon, and even when he talks the drumming thuds on.

The space we're in is a family-sized version of a high school locker room, and it's not a promising start when the toilet doesn't flush. "That'll be a serious problem later," I say, spotting the forty-eight beers and forty-eight soft drinks and bottled water laid out by the case in ice. It's enough for a picnic among neighbors, but Derek shakes his head at the small portions. "This won't do," he says as we help ourselves to beer and walk next door to have Polaroids taken for our full access passes.

When we're finished I ask Ripper if there's a pass that gets you into Sully's dressing room, too. "No way," he says. "It's off-limits except for the guy who has to decorate it before Sully goes in. The walls have to be covered with tapestries so that none of the cinderblock shows."

"Oh," I say, stuck for a moment.

"Sully has his ways," Ripper adds, as if that explains everything I might hear before the night is over.

But now, in the dressing room again, it's time for everyone to start worrying about Aaron like a parent. It's 7:08, both Ripper's and Derek's watches agree, and Aaron has just called to say he's lost "across the water," whatever that means. Ripper lays his cell phone down on the counter and stares at a computer screen that shows a map of Utica. Little by little he blows it up until it's so detailed I imagine it looks exactly like what a navigator sees before the launch of a smart bomb.

Ripper picks up the phone and gives instructions to Aaron to turn around and retrace his path. It's 7:12, and still there's just Jeremy drumming as accompaniment to Derek and me opening our second beers and Ripper sitting back to wait for his cell phone to ring again with the news of Aaron's next location.

Mark enters with the ease of somebody who doesn't know there's a crisis, but the phone rings, and when he sees Ripper hunch over the screen, he asks "What's up?" and gets the news.

"The last chapter of your book," he says. "You get to see us miss a show."

Nobody even smiles. They can start after 7:30, but each minute they're late is subtracted from their set, so if they go on at 7:45, they'll play four songs, an appearance so short I can't imagine Ben agreeing to do it.

"A left on Lafayette Street," Ripper says into the phone, studying the map. "That will take you to where you should be able to see the building. Go around back. I'll be there."

Ripper heads off at 7:17 as if he completely trusts the computer. If the detail were any larger, I think, we would see Aaron and Betty Jo's images on the screen.

By now Jeremy has put down his drumsticks and is using one of those stretch devices I used to see sold from the back pages of comic books. He pulls the cords open, then relaxes them. He pulls them again, repeating the sequence as if he wants to expand his chest for a shirtless performance.

Mark lays down paper towels on the floor, spacing them to fit where his hands go for a set of push ups. I think *vanity, biceps pumped,* but he talks as he does twenty, explaining it's to get his heart rate elevated so it's not a shock to his system when they go on. "If we do," he adds, Derek involuntarily glancing at his watch.

And then at 7:23 Aaron walks through the door, bearded now, dressed in jeans and a short-sleeved oxford shirt that looks as if it's been slept in. He suddenly looks nothing whatsoever like a modern rock guitarist, as if he's gearing up for a tryout as a banjo player in a rural country cover band.

For somebody who has to be on stage in seven minutes, he's calm as Betty Jo starts explaining about the slowest drivers in history clogging up the last sixty miles of two-lane.

A minute later Ben walks in wearing glasses, and I think, for a moment, he's dedicated, like Aaron, to a look that will discourage adoration by teenage girls. He seems pleased to see us, laughs when I say, "Last chance to look good in the book" as I tie my new laminate to my belt.

"We can't fuck up tonight then," he says, and now, at 7:25, he starts to put in his contact lenses while Betty Jo describes the horror of the one nonfunctioning toilet. "It will only get worse," I offer as she grits her teeth and closes the door.

"I know how to do this without touching anything," she says from inside the stall. "This isn't the time to fail."

"Ahhhhh," Ben groans, blinking in that way I've experienced a thousand times after inserting contact lenses into dry eyes. Five seconds later a buzzer set at civil-defense alert volume begins to grind through the closed door. "We're on," Ripper says, one more night of successful road-managing behind him. And because I'm closest to the door I lead the way like some radio station promotion winner, the listener who gets to live everything in the band's arena show life except performing on stage.

The audience is already roaring in the near-darkness as the amplified whining that signals "Home" will be the first song blares through the auditorium. Four different security guys let me pass without hesitation, and I slip into the aisle that runs between the crowd packed onto the arena floor and the people seated in the stands. Multiple spots run across the stage, and Breaking Benjamin goes on to a gratifying cheer from a crowd I guess is nearly five thousand. But thirty seconds into "Home" Aaron's guitar strap snaps as if it was worn out from the long drive. He pivots, steps back into the darkness, and reappears fifteen seconds later newly strapped in, the change happening as fast as a NASCAR pit stop.

In this first-of-three-bands format they have seven songs to generate enthusiasm and approval from several thousand people, most of whom likely don't know them or their music. I keep one eye on the fans halfway back who are just standing and watching through the first two songs, checking to see if their attitude changes. And I wonder if Aaron's new beard will be seen as something cute and lovable or something that labels him a hick.

When the band begins "Natural Life," turning to a heavier song, the crowd begins to come over to them. Moshers find pockets of space to slam in. Toward the back of the crowd fists begin to pump. Some people stand up by their seats. Ben works the crowd like an evangelist, screaming compliments between songs, picking out girls and giving them signs of approval, doing all the things that rock stars do to gain fans and change perception.

"Are you ready for some heavy shit?" Ben shouts, and a roar goes up as "Sugarcoat" starts. Four songs into the set I know Ben has given in to the necessity of touring with an aggressive high-profile band. The song he refused to perform a month before because it's so hard on his voice is the one that rouses the rest of the crowd with its hoarsely screamed choruses and relentless riff. Right now, thirty seconds into the song, I know Breaking Benjamin is being more successful than they were on the Jagermeister Tour. That Aaron, by the look of him flirting with the audience, striding across the stage, is enjoying this tour. That at least for another month he'll see the band as huge. And I know they're not going to play "Skin," their current single, the one we heard on the radio an hour outside of Utica; that, in fact, they're not going to play "Medicate," which is slated to be the next single, going for adds in June. That everything they're doing on stage is now designed to please as many people as possible in the Godsmack crowd.

Which works. Men wearing ball caps and tank tops fist pump for Breaking Benjamin. Women in low-cut blouses rock in place. Some of these people, I think, will spend money on Breaking Benjamin this week. When the crowd recognizes "Polyamorous," the set ends with appreciative lighters held aloft.

Before Cold, playing second, goes on, I wander with Aaron through the maze of trunks and monitors and cables behind the stage. "There's so much stuff back here," I say. "It looks like Godsmack is ready to invade a small country."

"They have seven trailers and six buses," Aaron says. "There's fifty-five people traveling with them as support staff. You'll see. They have everything going on. A lot of pyro."

"Really?" I say.

"These ceilings are metal, Dad," Aaron says at once. "These guys are pros."

We slip back into the dressing room for a new round of beers. "You see the ego ramps on the sides of the stage?" Jeremy asks. "Last week a girl climbed the scaffolding, jumped onto the stage and whispered in Mark's ear. 'I want to fuck you,' she said before security dragged her away."

Aaron leans against the wall beside the chair where I sit to take the pressure off my knees that are still screaming from five hours of driving. "You'll love this story, Dad," he says. "Saliva's equipment broke down when we were in Arizona."

Jeremy grins. I can tell he's as pleased as I am that Saliva had problems. "The second song," he says, "and all of a sudden their tape quit rolling."

"Did they tough it out?" I ask.

"No," Aaron says, and he finishes the story. "They just stopped when the tape broke. Josey Scott just stood there, and then they walked off until it was fixed. Definitely a highlight."

"You're right," I say. "I love that story." It's all I can do to not beam with smugness.

Ben is smiling and not drinking. "I'm trying to cut back," he says. "It's hard on my voice."

"You tempted to use the ego ramp?" I ask.

"Taboo," he says at once. "Sully only. Scooter from Cold went out on it the first night and caught shit."

"Never again?"

"Absolutely. Or else you're off the tour."

I'm as bored with Cold now as I was when Lifer opened for them, but Aaron tells me, between songs, that they've sold 101,000 CDs the first week out, opening at #3 on the Billboard chart. "Number three," he says. "Their manager was on the phone in minutes. They just moved to the main stage on Lollapalooza."

"They don't sound that good," I say.

"EJ does sound for them, did you know that?"

"Really? He's such a perfectionist."

"Yeah. So you know what's going on."

Godsmack, when they come on, is as much spectacle as music. The contents of all those trunks are suddenly on display. The stage is bookended by huge sets of what look like industrial-size cans that tower over the band. "Get ready, Dad," Aaron says, pointing to a spinning red light just off the stage. "This is going to be really loud."

And it is, the enormous Blam! that explodes from the stage making me duck in spite of myself. "Okay, that's it for a while," Aaron says, "but keep an eye out for that light. It'll tell you when percussion is coming again."

Godsmack's show is designed like a special effects blockbuster movie. The enormous percussion opening is followed by balls of flame, jets of propane driven upward from ten locations to ignition. I think of Great White and the Rhode Island disaster as the flames vanish near the ceiling, lean over to tell Aaron we should go out the exit behind the stage if disaster occurs.

"Sure," he says, but he tells me not to worry. "Enjoy," he adds.

"There's fire all night." And he's right about that;- soon a huge ball of flame erupts from the stylized sun that hangs above the band as they perform. "It's their symbol," Aaron says, but each time the flames disappear I examine the surface of that glittering sun, expecting it to be charred.

Fifteen minutes into the show, Sully, who looks to be barely five feet tall, runs up the ramp that ends ten feet from where we stand. He puts a bottle of water to his lips and then spits a mouthful onto the crowd below him. They raise their hands in salute, welcoming it. He spits again, and they roar. Whatever his affectations, Sully knows his audience.

"Sully has his own bus," Aaron says between songs. "It has a master bedroom that slides out from the side of the bus when it's parked."

I barely have time to raise my eyebrows before a woman rises on a hydraulic platform as Godsmack begins to play "Voodoo." The fireballs shoot up in earnest. She dances provocatively, dressed in the sort of tiny two-piece outfit that inspires forgetting the band. The multiple ascending fireballs, as they flash upward, seem so close to her and the nearby drummer that it's easy to imagine a disaster.

When I see the red light spinning I set my feet and shoulders. Blam! But this time the crowd flinches more than I do, though the roar that follows is loud enough to produce its own version of tinnitus.

"Four feet," Aaron says. "That's how close the closest flames are to the dancer and the drummer. And you know how you can feel the heat out in the audience."

I think he's exaggerating. Four feet sounds like she could inhale those flames as they rushed by. It sounds like instantaneous second-degree burns. I watch another set of fireballs, trying to estimate the distance for myself, and I'm sure it's ten feet or less, close enough for head shaking.

Back in the dressing room, Godsmack exiting to a sustained roar of unanimous approval, we're suddenly surrounded by a crowd of strangers, two of whom turn out to be members of Brand New Sin, the biker look-alikes from the first Saliva tour. Aaron introduces me to the burlier of the two, ignoring the crowd of women who have followed them in. "I saw you in State College," I say. "You kicked ass."

Sleeveless for maximum exposure of length-of-the-arms tattoos, he smiles. "Thanks," he says.

Five of the six women pull out what look to be identical metallic pipes that they light as casually as if they were smoking tobacco instead of marijuana. The sixth stays close to the stocky guy from Brand New Sin, and I guess wife or girlfriend; she beams when Aaron mentions Gavin. The conversation turns to the new baby of another Brand New Sin member and his wife, the room dividing into pot smoking and family conversation.

Finally, we move into a hallway behind the stage. E.J. shows up, complaining at once about the sound for Cold as if he recognized a problem but somehow wasn't responsible. Aaron pauses to talk with the guitarist from Cold, a man with a below-the-waist goatee and pink hair. As scary as he might appear on stage, up close he looks as mild-mannered as the front man for Cyphilis. And it pleases me that Aaron seems comfortable with him, that whatever distance there was between Cold and Lifer twenty months ago seems to have vanished.

And then a man with the skinniest legs I've ever seen stops to talk with Aaron. *Godsmack's drummer,* I think, because Aaron has told me he's freakishly thin and one of the best drummers on tour. I remember how demonstrative he was on stage, how big his flourishes made him seem, but here, in absurdly tight pants, he looks to have legs as thick as my own thin upper arms. Worse, they don't taper at the thighs, so it looks as if he has the kind of body you draw when you're in first grade. *Less than one hundred pounds,* I think, and yet he seems not at all self-conscious, as if having narrow pipe for legs is ordinary. And then Sully walks by trailed by an entourage, and nothing about his expression indicates he even recognizes Aaron.

Everything that follows feels like a hangover. An hour after the show, sitting on the tour bus, I feel like a chaperone. No one in the crowd even glances my way. At this hour, in this location, I'm not even a curiosity anymore. The bus, according to a sign posted, I'm sure, by Ripper, leaves at 4 A.M. There are three and a half hours to fill, and I don't have the stamina for any of the things that might fill them.

The band is less a part of it than the visitors. Ben is lost in video games. Jeremy smokes but, as always, doesn't drink. Mark withdraws, and Aaron is wrapped up in making sure Betty Jo is comfortable with driving home in the rain because she needs to be at work as a social studies teacher in the morning.

It's the rest of the crowd that's animated. The Brand New Sin guys keep talking up a possible show with Breaking Benjamin. They tell Aaron they're working on a better deal, wanting to leave Now or Never Records behind, and I remember searching in vain for spins of their single on any of the rock charts. All the women except the one who keeps talking about babies pack their pipes for another round. If the band gets a second wind at 1 A.M., I'm not going to see it. Derek and I are off to find a motel that won't start rolling down the highway at 4 A.M. I'm exhausted. I've lived as much of my son's rock and roll life as a father can.

A Rock and Roll Family Tree

Seed (1992–1994)
Matt Hayes, *Vocals*
Aaron Fincke / Noah Crowther (1992), *Guitar*
Dave Diers/Ethan Page (1992)/Matt Rhoads (1992)/
    Ethan Shaw (1993), *Bass*
Chris Lightcap/Jamie Markle (1992)/Andrew Stroko (1992), *Drums*

Epoch (1993–1997)
Ben Burnley, *Vocals/Guitar*
Rich Johnson (1993–1994)/Jason Divoli (1995–1997), *Guitar*
Roger Brennan (1993–1995)/Nick Hoover (1996–1997), *Bass*
Andrew Stroko, *Drums*

Strangers With Candy (1999–2000)
Nick Coyle, *Vocals*
Aaron Fincke, *Guitar*
Tony Kruzka, *Turntables*
Nick Hoover (1999)/Mark Klepaski (1999–2000), *Bass*
Chris Lightcap, *Drums*

Plan 9 (1999–2001)

Ben Burnley, *Vocals/Guitar*
Brian Fitzgerald (2000), *Guitar*
Jason Divoli (1999)/Andy Seal (2000)/John Price (2001), *Bass*
Jeremy Hummel, *Drums*

Driver/Lifer/MyDownfall (2000–2003)

Nick Coyle, *Vocals*
Aaron Fincke (2000–2002)/Derek Spencer (2002–2003), *Guitar*
Tony Kruzka (2000–2002), *Turntables*
Mark Klepaski (2000–2001)/Ian Wiseman(2001–2003), *Bass*
Chris Lightcap, *Drums*

Breaking Benjamin (1998) (2001–)

Ben Burnley, *Vocals/Guitar*
Aaron Fincke (1998; 2001–), *Guitar*
Mark Klepaski (2001–)/Nick Hoover (1998)/John Price (2001), *Bass*
Jeremy Hummel(2001–)/Chris Lightcap (1998), *Drums*

Afterword

If the average signed band lasts eighteen months, the more than seven months that have passed since the Godsmack show in Utica represent about 40 percent of the hamster-like lifespan of rock and roll. So Breaking Benjamin, nearly twenty-two months after being signed, has already beaten the odds, because now, in late December, they are recording their second CD, not yet broken up or dropped by their label.

There's pressure, of course, for the next CD to sell more than the 200,000 copies *Saturate* has managed to scan so far. The record label wants a hit single, and for two months now Aaron has played demos for me every time he's come home from New York City, where Breaking Benjamin is recording this time. Each time, after a song ends, he announces that I've just heard one more potential single Hollywood has rejected.

Ben has even spent time writing songs with Billy Corgan, who made a name for himself with Smashing Pumpkins, and a few days before Christmas Aaron plays this five-song set in my kitchen. The songs sound plaintive and more mainstream. They sound like songs that should be pushed to the Contemporary Hits format, tunes that might compete for a place among what most people think of as Top Forty. Some of them, Aaron has assured me, are going to make the CD; one of them may be that first, elusive single, or if not, definitely the second.

"Skin," their second single, has just logged in at #76 on the Radio and Records 2003 Active Rock Top 100, ten slots below where

"Polyamorous" finished in 2002, but besides sales and airplay, what else can happen in seven months to a band that came off tour in June and hasn't had a single on national radio since July?

For starters, the members can resume their personal lives. Aaron can throw a party for Gavin's second birthday, complete with a costumed Cookie Monster and Elmo, who both tower over his fascinated face. He can remodel his house and put in a lawn. He can bring Gavin to my house, and we can go to a circus or a playground. He and Betty Jo can become closer. He can buy a yellow lab puppy and name him Sonny, that dog following us from house to house as Gavin learns the joys of trick-or-treating.

The others? Mark's daughter has a first birthday, and Jeremy, who, astonishingly, has successfully given up his heavy cigarette habit, gets married. Ben, who seldom buys anything except pizza and video games, even purchases a car, although it's a used, purple Pontiac Grand-Am, not quite what fans would expect to see parked in a rock singer's driveway. And to show that long shots can enter the same spot in the bulls-eye of coincidence, when Aaron and I take Gavin to the first scholastic football game either of us has attended since he graduated from high school, Jeremy and his wife Yvette are there, too, half of Breaking Benjamin sitting unrecognized for two hours in the bleachers of their former school.

To stay in the public eye the band does some spot shows, including one at the Bryce Jordan Center in State College, a huge venue where they open for the Deftones. It's the most heavily policed show I've ever attended. Even someone like me is patted down by security. There seem to be as many ushers as there are at major league baseball games, and they insist on people sitting in their assigned seats, so for the first time in four years I sit in a chair to watch my son perform.

It feels odd, especially when Butch and his friends are right beside Derek and me, and they all obediently remain seated as well. It's almost surprising when the crowd around us, when Breaking Benjamin comes on, responds by cheering like sports fans. Less than a minute into the show, however, I'm distracted by the couple in front of us, both of whom begin head banging.

I mean serious head banging. They grip the hand rail (they're in Row A), heave themselves forward and back, somehow gauging the distance so precisely they throw themselves to the extreme without slamming themselves into concussion or unconsciousness against the railing. Both the man and the woman show flexibility and endurance.

More than half an hour later, they're still in motion, the happiest couple, I think, in the auditorium. And beside them sit two young men who never move during the entire set, neither of them even changing expressions or shifting in their seats. I think they hate Breaking Benjamin until they maintain that demeanor right through the Deftones' performance.

A month later I manage to convince a friend who is my age to attend a headlining show, doubling the number of over-fifty men in the club, which is so crowded I have to fend off fans with both forearms to maintain a space to stand. "It's something," he says, finding his own bit of slack in the crowd, a place from which to see for himself what I've been periodically describing to him for nearly four years.

Meanwhile, the Wilkes-Barre dream show happens, My Downfall opening for Breaking Benjamin, the crowd roaring when Nick appears on stage, standing beside Aaron to sing with Ben. By early November, though, Nick leaves My Downfall, hooking up with two former members of Filter to form a new band called WideScreen. He heads for Chicago, excited to front a band that has an excellent chance, because of its pedigree, to be signed. It's the end of the Strangers With Candy/Lifer part of the rock and roll family tree, and Chris, Ian, and Derek are abruptly out of work.

But I want to avoid an afterword of simple summary, so when Breaking Benjamin headlines two shows just before New Year's, I have Aaron put me on the guest list and drive.

The first show is at The Staircase, the familiar Wilkes-Barre venue, and I'm barely inside when I see Tony, who looks to have even more facial piercings than he had in the spring, so many, in fact, I have to work at keeping eye contact instead of counting them, knowing, regardless, that the number is well into double figures. I ask him about his band Good Grief and whether the CD they were working on nine months ago is finished, and he shrugs.

It's an awkward moment, but I'm rescued when Hyland throws his arms around me like an old friend. Before long, I see Butch, who's gaining weight in his new life as a married man, and Jim, Aaron's friend, who seems to be at every show. When I realize there's no VIP section roped off, I head downstairs to stand with the teenagers, forgoing the bar for a line of sight.

Larry, the manager, is at the bottom of the stairs right where he stands for every Staircase show. We shake hands, and I tell myself his presence is reassuring, that he wouldn't be here just as he was for earlier shows unless Breaking Benjamin was still a viable commercial rock band.

How fragile I've come to think this world is, and it's reinforced when Brand New Sin, opening for Breaking Benjamin, announces they're "between labels." I remember at once Aaron's prophecy, how Now or Never Records wouldn't have the clout to get spins for Brand New Sin's first single. The front man however, is as aggressive as he was when I first saw the band in January. "Who got a blow job for Christmas?" he asks the crowd, all of whom, on this floor, are under twenty-one.

Before Breaking Benjamin comes on, I move up near the sound board, where there's always an open area blocked off. Just to my right, a guy with the same idea pushes forward, and I notice he has a bar code tattoo on the back of his neck. *What does he cost?* I think. And then it occurs to me that although it's the first one I've seen, a bar code tattoo is probably not that original.

Fortunately, just to my left, Chris has had the same idea, so I have a chance to ask him what's happened in his life since My Downfall broke up. "I'm the production manager for an R&B guy named Anthony Hamilton," he says. "It's been pretty cool so far."

I think *roadie,* but as he talks, it sounds as if he has responsibility, something to keep him on the road and in the business, and I'm relieved that he hasn't said "nothing much." I wish him well and mean it, remembering his college freshman essay from what is now eight years ago, how the most important thing in his life was being "in music."

He tells me that the WideScreen project, or at least Nick's involvement in it, has collapsed, that Nick is back home without ever playing a gig or recording a song. "It depends on who you listen to," Chris says, explaining the reasons for the failure by suggesting Nick isn't blameless. And he tells me Derek, the guitarist who replaced Aaron, has sold his equipment now that My Downfall has broken up, and that he doesn't know what Ian, the bass player, is doing.

Freddie, the morning deejay who did so much to hype Breaking Benjamin in the early days, walks up and extends his hand. "How you doing, Mr. Fincke?" he says, so polite and soft spoken I think, for a moment, I've mistaken him for someone other than the Howard

Stern–like emcee of the drive time show for northeast Pennsylvania. He's on his way to do the intro, replaced, a moment later, by two guys who represent The Shallow Bay, the best fan site for Breaking Benjamin on the Internet, and they're so enthusiastic and eager they give off the vibe of door-to-door fundamentalists.

Although the audience goes crazy like it always does when the band plays close to home, the show itself seems oddly routine, and I have to remind myself that for those who don't see the band over and over again like I do, hearing all the songs on the CD plus three songs from the upcoming CD is exhilarating.

Afterwards? The band exchanges late Christmas presents before they pack up and quickly leave. Two married couples, one steady couple, and Ben with a new girlfriend. "Not like the days of Strangers with Candy," Derek says. *Not like the days of Lifer either,* I think. Anyone who imagines Breaking Benjamin starting an all-night party would be as inaccurate as their fantasies about the lifestyle suggested by the outlaw-biker persona of Brand New Sin.

But that's Wilkes-Barre, home territory, and I worry the next night when I drive with Derek and my daughter's husband David to Lancaster and a venue, The Chameleon, where they've never played. On Christmas morning Aaron had announced there were twenty-eight tickets presold so far, a number that suggested the club might be as empty as a pre-MTV Strangers With Candy venue.

So I'm relieved when the club, which looks to hold five or six hundred, is already full ninety minutes before they go on. We stand at the bar upstairs with Aaron, who no one seems to recognize here, even the drunk guy with a mustache and a pony tail and a tank top who steps out of a rock and roll comic book to tell us, unsolicited, that both warm-up bands have sucked so far and that he's sure the third will suck as well, that Breaking Benjamin "fucking doesn't suck" and that's why he's here.

Aaron looks puzzled, and for the only time in four years, I hear him tell a stranger he's "in the band," which surprises me but doesn't faze the drunk guy because he's ranting about how great Breaking Benjamin is, trying to convince us we should appreciate this opportunity to hear and see them. When the pony-tailed guy finally moves on, I predict he'll scream "You suck" every time the next band leaves dead air between songs. Nobody disagrees. "He's The Heckler," David says. "It's his mission."

Just then, a three-year-old boy runs by. A moment later, a woman follows. An employee, I think. A mother stuck without a babysitter. The boy is barely older than Gavin, and Aaron frowns. "What's up with that?" he asks me, and a few minutes later, when it becomes obvious the woman is there as a fan, buying a Coke at the bar to share with the small boy and working her way into a spot from which to watch the last opening band, I have to agree. Hearing loss, I think. Physical injury. Five minutes later, when the band pauses after their first song, the pony-tailed guy, from just behind the three-year-old boy, screams "You suck!" so loudly the room goes quiet.

"Well," Aaron says, "that's getting to the point," and three successive songs are punctuated by a "You suck!" from The Heckler before Aaron nods and disappears down the back stairs to the dressing room behind the stage.

It's time to work our way into position for Breaking Benjamin. Jim, Aaron's friend, has a spot blocked out just behind The Heckler that pleases everybody, and I slip in beside a guy who turns out to be the program manager for 105.7, the X, the modern rock station for the Harrisburg/Lancaster/York area. "Have you ever seen Breaking Benjamin before?" he asks, and I smile.

"A lot," I say. "The guitarist is my son."

He shakes my hand and looks at me curiously. "Is he one of the ones who was in Lifer?" he asks.

"Yes," I say, and he relaxes.

"You know Freddie, don't you?" he says. "He called me when the Lifer CD came out to push for it. 'Cut these guys a break,' he kept saying, but I thought it was too raw to play except after midnight."

Raw? I remember the heavy songs by Papa Roach and Disturbed and Korn in heavy rotation on his station during the months that Lifer was fighting for air time. That excuse makes me wonder if Universal ever plugged Lifer to 105.7, the X, whether a push from the label could have taken the edges off enough to get spins during the day and early evening. I think back to "Boring," and it strikes me that it wasn't radio listeners, but this program manager and a hundred others just like him who had decided the popularity and sales of Lifer.

"Everything could have been otherwise." Jim Harrison, one of my favorite fiction writers, plays off this phrase near the end of his recent memoir *Off to the Side*. "Yes, it could have," I think, and now this phrase flutters over the possibilities of the next few months. The CD will be finished in January. Though these things are always subject to delays, the first single is scheduled for early March, the CD release for mid-April. There's no question the career of Breaking Benjamin will be sustained or destroyed by sales that will be tracked closely through the late spring and early summer. For starters, I'm certain, the numbers need to be "more than Saturate's."

Even this book about rock and roll is put to the test of public perception. The title, since I began writing it, has always been *Kicking Ass,* yet now, as the copy is being prepared for printing, that title has been rejected because it's likely to discourage a "mature audience."

Too raw, I think, not agreeing, but willing to work up a list of dozens of alternate titles, all of which I reject myself before I submit them because they're inappropriate, clichéd, or obscure. Standing here with the program manager, I know that only hours before I decided on *Come With It Now,* the call to arms from the beginning of Rage Against the Machine's "Bulls on Parade," and that Derek, who writes advertising copy, subsequently told me half the audience wouldn't get it.

"Amped," he said, and as soon as I heard the word, I knew it was going to be the title.

"It has the multiple meanings I want for any title," I said, and Derek nodded.

"And it's what you are before every show," he added, and I didn't disagree.

But now here I am turning toward the stage when Breaking Benjamin comes on to an enormous, gratifying roar, including a scream from The Heckler, who immediately goes over the top with enthusiasm. He and his friend sing every word, rock violently in place through each song, and raise their hands in salute when they end. As the prelude to "Water" begins, they raise the shots of Jagermeister they've had in front of them for half an hour and down them simultaneously, perfectly choreographed to the first heavy riff. "Yes!" they scream, and I think "props to the Heckler," who finally dances so hard in place he begins to leave the floor in a sort of ecstasy so intense I imagine him flinging himself over the railing to consummate this extended foreplay.

The show ends with "Shallow Bay." Aaron has a lengthy solo in the middle now, well over a minute of improvisation that rivets me. I remember him telling me how much better musically the new CD will be, how much more ambitious it is, how many more effects are in it, how much more "real playing" he gets to do, and I hear and see the joy he has in performing as well as he can. "It's going to be more an album by the band all together than the first one," he's said, and I know that this solo is representative, that work like this makes him feel he has more of a stake in the band.

Finally, after Breaking Benjamin walks offstage, there's the inevitable "One More Song" chant, the room loud with unison voices.

But it sounds different in another town. We're not in Wilkes-Barre or Scranton, and yet it sounds and looks unanimous, a rhythmic chant that sustains itself longer than I think it can. And then there's a slapping of hands on tables and railings. A stomping of feet so loud and insistent that it sounds like a call for a ninth inning rally, the home team needing one more hit to win the pennant. The chant and the drumming go on and on. It doesn't seem to matter what happens as long as Breaking Benjamin reappears. 2004 is about to begin; for a moment it feels as if these voices and bodies will keep this up for twenty-four hours, welcoming in whatever comes next.